THE BABES IN THE WOOD

A Basic Pantomime

by

S. A. POLLEY and CONRAD CARTER

SAMUEL FRENCH

LONDON

EW YORK SYDNEY TORONTO HOLLYWOOD

PRINTED IN GREAT BRITAIN BY
BUTLER & TANNER LTD, FROME AND LONDON

PREFACE.

Of all our national forms of entertainment, the Pantomime is perhaps the most traditional and shows least signs of waning popularity. The average " run " of the professional pantomime is certainly as long as ever, and for many years it has been a source of considerable enjoyment and profit among amateur societies.

It is for this latter field of activity that this series of " BASIC PANTOMIME " has been specially designed, both as regards the " scripts," the settings, and the general production problems which face every company in work of this type.

Apart from the time-honoured stories on which all our pantomimes are (and rightly) based, much of their success depends on topicality, local and current humour, and by no means least upon the songs and choruses of the time—even of the year.

With this in view, these " basic " pantomimes have been prepared, not as the final, unalterable show, but as *bases* upon which may be built the ultimate product according to the desires, and the resources, of the individual company.

The scripts follow, in each case, the traditional stories very strictly. Any major departure would be resented by the youngest—and the oldest !—members of the audience. The dialogue is in modern prose, and prepared so that "cuts," additions, and the introduction of "local" or "topical" references may be effected with a minimum of difficulty.

Simplicity has been the prior aim also with regard to the settings, which are dealt with in detail in the "Production Notes" for each of the scripts. These contain suggestions for yet further simplification where the exigencies of the theatre are exceptionally limited, as well as indications of elaboration for those who are more fortunately placed.

Equal consideration has been given to the matter of Musical Numbers, Dances, etc. Those indicated represent what may be regarded as a reasonable minimum ; in fact, where resources are available, one or two extra numbers might be added with advantage. But the basic form which the pantomimes take render these additions quite easy to effect.

On the other hand, it will be found that, if desired, the pantomimes may be produced without alteration in any department despite the title of "BASIC" which has, for the foregoing reasons, been conferred upon them.

THE BABES IN THE WOOD

CHARACTERS:

BARON HUGO BACQUE.

SKRIBB (his Steward).

OGBERT
EGBERT } (his retainers).

DAME TRUFORM (the Old Woman who Lived in a Shoe).

CLARENCE (her husband).

JOLIJAK (her eldest son).

LILLI
SKINNA } (her twin daughters).

CHERRYBLOSSOM (another daughter).

BLAKEY (another son).

DIB and
DOLLY } (The Babes).

A SEA CAPTAIN.

THE LANDLORD OF THE DOODROP INN.

HIS WIFE.

THE FAIRY OF GOOD INTENT.

Other Children of Dame Truform.

Villagers, Townspeople, Tradespeople, etc.

Bathing Girls and Boys.

Ballet of Rabbits, Robins, Squirrels.

vi

SCENES.

MUSICAL NUMBERS.

Act I.

Scene 1.

No. 1. Opening Chorus
  (*Chorus of Tradespeople and Villagers*)

  2. Duet : " We're Ogbert and Egbert "
  (Ogbert, Egbert, Chorus)

  3. Comedy Mime
  (*Tradespeople*, Baron, Skribb, *Retainers*)

  4. Trio (Dame, Jolijak, Sea Captain)

Scene 2.

No. 5. Quartette (Dib, Dolly, Ogbert, Egbert)

Scene 3.

No. 6. Duet .. .. (Dib *and* Dolly)
  7. Ballet of Robins

Scene 5.

No. 8. Reprise of No. 6 (Dib *and* Dolly)
  9. Ensemble Number
  (Cherryblossom *and Company*)

Act II.

Scene 1.

No. 10. Song .. .. (Dame *and Chorus*)
  11. Quartette
  (Dame, Clarence. Ogbert, Egbert)

Scene 3.

No. 12. Opening Chorus(Clarence *and* Children)
  13. Boating Chorus .. (Full Company)

PRODUCTION NOTES.

Although there are a few more scenes than in some of the BASIC PANTOMIMES, the number of different settings have been, of course, kept to a minimum. Five of the settings are used twice, and all of these are very quickly re-set. A good deal of the scenery can be kept set throughout the show without "striking", as will be apparent on studying these notes and the GROUND PLANS.

Act I. *Scene* 1.

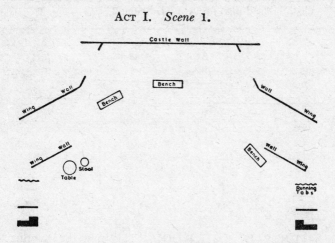

Back stage, a cloth, or flats if preferred, to represent castle walls. Two wall wings on either side, giving wide entrances down stage, and somewhat narrower entrances upstage into the castle interior. On a stage of fair size only the downstage wings need be struck. This setting is used for the final scene of Act Three, and the back-cloth may remain throughout.

Act I. *Scene* 2.

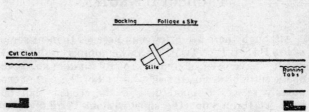

This is a front cloth, with a central cut and a foliage backing. In the gap C., a wooden stile is placed. This cloth is used also for Act II, Scene 2.

Act I. *Scene* 3.

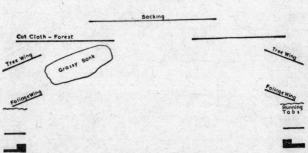

DEEP IN THE WOOD. This may be another cloth at half stage depth, showing foliage and trees. There are foliage and tree wings to provide exits. If it is possible, there should be a central cut in the cloth with an additional entrance there. Also, a small sloping bank up R.C., covered with artificial grass, will be an advantage, to serve as a resting place for the BABES. Do not strike, as this set is used again in Scene 5.

Act I. *Scene 4.*

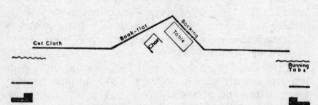

THE BARON'S STUDY. This is another front cloth with a central cut and backing. Or, two plain masking wings, with a book wing at C. In the recessed opening at C., a table and chair to convey the impression of the study.

Act I. *Scene 5.* As in Scene 3.

Act II. *Scene 1.*

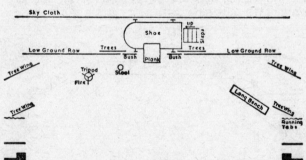

DAME TRUFORM'S BOWER. This is a three-quarter set. It will consist of a plain sky-cloth, and, at a little distance below it, a low ground row and tree pieces, to convey the impression that a river flows between this and the cloth.

At the edge of the " bank," at C., is the Shoe.

This should be as large as possible and partly hidden by trees. There should be an opening in the Shoe and an exit on the prompt side of it, so that characters entering the Shoe may disappear convincingly into its mysterious depths. There should be a gang-plank to lead from the bank to the Shoe, which is supposed to be floating on the water.

If possible, the Shoe should be mounted on a very low truck with wheels, so that it may appear to float away at the end of Scene 3 of this Act. Alternatively, it will be quite effective if the shoe rocks slightly, or can be somewhat withdrawn away from the bank further upstage. This scene is not struck, as it is used very soon after in Scene 3.

ACT II. *Scene* 2. ON THE WAY TO THE WOOD. Same as ACT I, Scene 2.

ACT II. *Scene* 3. Same as Scene 1.

During the Interlude in front of tabs after Scene 3, the Bower set must be struck, except for the sky-cloth. We now have :—

ACT II. *Scene* 4.

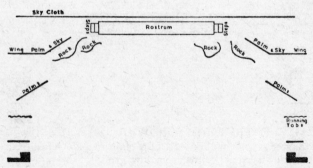

THE BEACH at BERM-on-SEA. This consists of the sky-cloth from the previous scene, and some palm and rock wings to provide entrances R. and L. If possible, a low rostrum back C., with low rocks below it. Also, one or two low rocks for sitting purposes would be an advantage.

Act III. *Scene 1.*

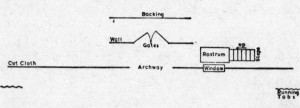

THE CASTLE GATES. This should be a cut-cloth at about half stage depth. There should be a central archway cut, with a stone wall backing, with an iron gate, to open (or heavy doors). If preferred, the gate or doors may be flush with the cloth. There is a window fairly high up, cut in the cloth L. of the centre. Steps must be placed behind this window so that the BABES may be seen looking out, and their faces must be lit from within.

Act III. *Scene 2.*

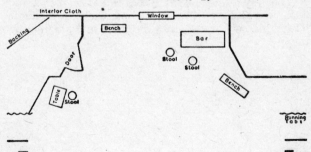

THE DOODROP INN. This has already been set behind the Sc. 1. cloth. It may consists of a cloth, or interior flats at the back, with a window represented. One interior wing each side will serve, that on the R. having a door. This setting will be struck during Scene 3, which is the simple front cloth used in Scene 1.

Act III. *Scene* 3. As in Scene 1.

Act III. *Scene* 4. THE CASTLE COURTYARD. As in Act I, Scene 1. The back flats (or cloth) have remained set throughout. It is merely necessary to re-set the side wings during Scene 3.

———

The interludes during scene changes are clearly indicated in the book as they occur. A special list of Furniture and Properties is provided. There are no difficult " magical " effects. The thistle, cobweb, etc., can, if desired, be acted by children so disguised.

Some difficulty may be found as to the " Horse." It is not essential that the Babes ride it on stage, and if this is not insisted on, the horse becomes a simple matter, namely, two actors in the usual stage-horse disguise.

THE BABES IN THE WOOD

ACT ONE.

PROLOGUE.

House lights out. Floats NIL. In a spot, C., the FAIRY OF GOOD INTENT appears before the curtain, to soft music which dies away as she speaks.

FAIRY. A word with you—just as you settle down !
    Mine is the power to charm away a frown.
    For that, you came—to lose your many cares,
    To be transported far from your affairs,
    Be made to laugh, to sing, to see the old
    Quaint story played of Babes and Baron bold.
    Mine is the power to bring these to your eyes,
    Mine is the power ! And, as you may surmise,
    Mine is the pleasure, too—to give you this delight,
    As you will see, if you watch close to-night.
    What matter if the Baron Bacque on evil deeds is bent ?
    He has to reckon yet with *me*—the Fairy Good Intent . . .

(She pauses. Then, with a saucy smile) . . . Good-night!

BLACK OUT. MUSIC. *Floats and other lighting up as the curtain rises on . . .*

SCENE 1.

SCENE.—*The Courtyard of the Castle of* BARON HUGO.

The main castle walls are at the back. Arched entrances to the interior up R. and up L. Wider entrances down R. and down L. to the outer world. A bench or two, and a small table with a chair.

(SEE THE GROUND PLAN.)

The courtyard is filled with townspeople and tradesmen laden with wares for sale to the BARON.

During the opening music there is a good deal of movement and business, laughter, and so on.

Then the Chorus *go into :—*

No. 1. Opening No. (*Ensemble. To the air of* " *The Lass of Richmond Hill.*")

Ensemble.	We've come to sell the Baron Bacque
	Whatever he may need
	His mighty larder must not lack
	To satisfy his greed !
Butcher.	This tender meat
Baker.	My bread so sweet
Dairyman.	Pure milk and eggs new laid
Woman.	He'll always try
	My apple pie
Ensemble.	But shall we e'er be paid ?
	Ah, shall we e'er be paid ?
	Not yet, we are afraid !
	He lives on tick
	It makes us sick
	To fear we'll ne'er be paid !
Draper.	The silk and velvet I've to sell
	Will grace his bulky torso
Shoemaker.	These boots and shoes of polish smell
Small Boy.	And so does he—but more so !
Greengrocer.	My turnips fine—
Wine Merchant.	This cask of wine—
Apothecary.	The pills that I have made !
Fruiterer.	These pears are ripe
Butcher.	And so's my tri-ipe !
Ensemble.	But shall we e'er be paid ?
	Ah, shall we e'er be paid ?
	No, never, we're afraid !
	He lives on tick
	It makes us sick
	To know we'll ne'er be paid !

(Dance. *This is interrupted by the entrance of* Ogbert *and* Egbert, *two retainers, who rush on up L.*)

Ogbert (*pushing his way through the crowd*). Here— I say ! What's this ? What's this ?

EGBERT. Pass along, please ! (*They try to drive the crowd into line upstage.*)

CHORUS (*together, ad lib.*). Market day ! It's market day ! We've come to sell the Baron . . .

OGBERT. Sell the Baron ? I didn't know he was for sale. (*To* EGBERT.) Have you heard anything about this ?

EGBERT. They mean—sell—him—things.

OGBERT. Then why can't they say so ? Anyway, we can't have potatoes all over the courtyard. It isn't as if they were chips . . . are we frying tonight ? (*To the* CROWD.) Anyway, get back—get back ! (*pushing the crowd back*).

EGBERT. Come along—come along ! (*pulling the crowd forward*).

OGBERT. Don't keep coming along when I'm getting back or they'll be coming back while we're getting along !

EGBERT. Anyway, make a line—make a line ! The Baron'll be here in a minute ! (*Bus. with* CROWD.)

OGBERT. Hi, there ! You with a haddock. If you're a fishmonger—you ought to know your plaice !

(OGBERT *and* EGBERT *roar with laughter.* CROWD *do not even smile. The retainers notice this.*)

EGBERT (*shouting*). Well, anyway, keep your prices low this morning, because his temper's high . . .

(OGBERT *and* EGBERT *start to fall into each other's arms with laughter again, but check on seeing the unsmiling faces.*)

OGBERT. And no tricks please, or he'll belabour. . .

EGPERT. Bludgeon . . .

OGBERT. Butcher . . .

EGBERT. And BUST . . .

BUTCHER (*coming forward*). Who are you with your belabouring bludgeoning butchering busting . . . you've got a lot of bees in your bonnet, haven't you ? Who are you, anyway ?

EGBERT (*to* OGBERT). Shall we tell him ?

OGBERT (*girlishly*). Oh, do let's !

EGBERT. He must be new round here.

OGBERT. One of those people from the Council Houses at (*local town*). Let's put him wise.

(*The* CROWD *gather round.*) *They go into :—*

No. 2. "We're Ogbert and Egbert." (OGBERT, EGBERT, *and* CHORUS.) (*To the Air of* "*Are you Mr. Reilly ?* ")

BOTH. We're Ogbert and Egbert, retainers of course.

We're servants and soldiers and trainers of horse.

We're Ogbert and Egbert

At dirty work egspert

CROWD. And never a trace on your face of remorse !

(*Chanting, with sinister steps*)

OGBERT *and* EGBERT. Yah—ha ! B-r-r-r-*chee !*

EGBERT. I'm Egbert—he's Ogbert—our crime is refined

OGBERT. Though weird are our beards and our faces are lined

EGBERT. Our lives are one fiddle

OGBERT. Black Markets we diddle

CROWD. And to cheating at Ludo you're also inclined !

(*Chanting, with sinister steps*) :

OGBERT *and* EGBERT. Yah—ha ! B-r-r-r-*chee !*

OGBERT. I'm Ogbert—he's Egbert—we have our soft spots,

We sing to our children asleep in their cots,

We wangle the kitty

But love a good ditty

CROWD. If it's dealing with stealing and murderous plots !

(*Chanting with sinister steps*) :

OGBERT *and* EGBERT. Yah—ha ! B-r-r-r-*chee !*

(CROWD *retreat.*)

OGBERT *and* EGBERT. We're Egbert and Ogbert—
our natures are pure
Our curious habits we never shall cure !
CROWD. Whatever their ending
You won't catch 'em bending
Their glorious story will ever endure !
ENSEMBLE (*fortissimo*). YAH—HA ! B-R-R-R-
CHEE !

OGBERT (*pressing the crowd back*). Now, that's
enough—that's enough ! Here comes the Baron !
EGBERT. The Baron ! Take yer 'ats off, can't yer ?
OGBERT. Kaindly remove your head-gear !

(CHORD.)

(CROWD *all doff hats and bow, curtsy, etc., as the* BARON
enters up L., followed by SKRIBB, *a thin, wheezy
Steward.*)

BARON (*striding down C.*). Ten thousand blisters !
What infernal clatter !
What want you, villains, with this senseless chatter ?
SKRIBB. 'Tis market day, and so they've called to
barter.
Your custom, lord, is really what they're arter !
BARON. Great Yarmouth ! How can I be expected
to attend to housekeeping when my head's in a whirl ?
What do I pay you for ?
SKRIBB. Well, it's some time since you paid me—
I've forgotten. However, in view of the approach of
the election to the local Drains Committee, I think it
would be advisable to show a little friendliness.
BARON. What ? Oh, yes ! Here—you scum—, I
should say, good people, what have you to offer ?

(*The music of "* The Keel Row *" starts, and* CHORUS
go into a MIME *while the* BARON, SKRIBB, OGBERT
and EGBERT *go up and down the lines, choosing
things, which the last two named have to carry.*)

No. 3. COMEDY MIME. (*Full Company.*)
(*Air :* " *The Keel Row.*")

EGBERT (*to orchestra : eventually*). Don't play it again. I couldn't carry another parsnip !

OGBERT (*carrying a side of beef*). Oh that this too, too solid flesh would melt. It's a long lane that breaks the camel's back.

(*They both stagger off.*)

BARON. Well, that's all, good people—and good day to you. My steward will pay you—

ALL. Ah ! Yes ! (*they move to* SKRIBB).

BARON. Next week !

(*Terrific crash off L.* EGBERT *hurries on L.*).

BARON. What was that ?

EGBERT. It's all right, my lord. He said he couldn't see where he was going. He was quite right—he couldn't.

BARON. The marketing is ended. Close the castle gates.

(OGBERT *enters L. rather battered.*)

EGBERT. Oh—there you are ! You heard, didn't you ? Cer-lose the castle gates ! Come on !

(*They go up through the crowd, then they dash back.*)

EGBERT.   Oh—no !

OGBERT.   Oh—yes !

BARON.   What's this ?

EGBERT.   I quite forgot. A party without.

BARON.   A party ? Without what ?

EGBERT.   Without the portcullis.

BARON.   I never ordered one. Who is it ?

EGBERT.   A woman.

OGBERT.   A female.

BARON.   A female woman ?

EGBERT.   Yea ! With a boy.

OGBERT.   She craves a boon.

BARON. A boon ? A plain boon **or a currant boon ?**

EGBERT.   She has a suit to press.

BARON. What does she take us for ? The (. . .) Valet Service ? Quick, villains ! Do my bidding—tell her to go !

EGBERT. You go.

OGBERT. No—you go. No, Baron Hugo—he go.

BARON. Tell her to *go* !

EGBERT ⎫ (*Together, shouting at each other*).   **TELL**
OGBERT ⎭   **HER TO GO** !

DAME (*heard off*). What's that I hear ? Tell her to go ?

EGBERT and OGBERT (*together*). The party comes, my lord !

(*They turn and run round behind the crowd, down L.*)

DAME TRUFORM (*entering R. through the crowd*). Tell her to *go*? Go ? Was that the word ? After I've been sitting on a block of stone for half an hour cooling my heels. Go, indeed ! And that's justice, is it ? Where *is* the Baron ?

SKRIBB (*advancing to R.C.*). Hush—hush—there he is !

DAME. What do you mean—hush, hush ? I don't want to know his Christian name—I'll give him a better one in a minute.

BARON (*to L.C.*). Woman—what is this ?

DAME. Don't you call me a woman ! Oh—I beg your pardon—you're the Baron. Yes—you must be. I recognise the plated necktie. Good morning. Excuse my little bit of temperament, but if I don't get a friendly greeting, well, you know what girls are !

BARON. Do you know to whom you speak ?

DAME. Oh, rather—I've found the big noise at last, but I'd like to have a word with your commissionaire who told me you'd only be five minutes. Do you know, I got so annoyed, counting the minutes, I dropped my hour glass, and now I've lost all count of time—so I suppose I shall have to give up my singing . . . and speaking of singing . . .

BARON. Stop ! Stop ! What do you want of me ?

DAME. Ah—how nice of you to make it a personal

matter. Well—since you put it like that—I want you to have a look at my son.

BARON. Your son? Is he worth looking at?

DAME (*simpering*). Oh yes, he's the very *image* of his *mother*! I'll fetch him in!

(*She turns and shouts off R.*)

Joli! Joli!

BARON. Oh—this is intolerable!

(JOLIJAK—*a bright young lad—runs on L.*)

JOLIJAK. Yes, ma? (*He pays little attention, but turns and jokes with the girls.—Bus.*)

DAME. Here he is, Mr. Baron, dear. There—doesn't he do me credit? Eighteen—and never given his mother a moment's anxiety. (*Aside to* JOLIJAK) Stand still, you little maggot, or I'll knock your head off.

BARON. But what—

DAME. Oh, dear—I was just coming to that. Though it tears my heart to part with him—(*aside*) Smile, can't you? (*To the* BARON) Yet I must! I must find him a job. And what better than in the Castle?

BARON. A job—in my service?

DAME. Just the very thing, Mr. Baron. And in one of your lovely uniforms!

BARON. My good woman! Skribb—tell her!

SKRIBB. Woman! Can't you read?

(*He points to NO HANDS WANTED notice on the wall at the back.*)

DAME. Oh, yes—I saw that—but that don't matter. My boy's so handy with his feet.

BARON. No—and No!

DAME. But if you'll just let me speak for a *moment*—

BARON. No—and No!

DAME. But—

BARON. No—no—and No to you!

DAME. Well, Postlethwaite and Postlethwaite and Postlethwaite to *you*!

BARON. Send this rabble away and CLOSE THE GATES!

(*He strides off L.*)

DAME. And no smoking in the lifts ! Rabble indeed ! Well, if this is Baron's Court, give me Hammersmith !

JOLIJAK. Come, mother, the gentleman said "No."

DAME. Yes, in triplicate ! Well, he's done for himself—he's done for himself ! If ever I get the chance to do that toad in the hole a nasty turn . . .

SKRIBB. Silence ! That is treason !

DAME. And who might you be ?

SKRIBB (*shouting at her*). Steward !

DAME. No thank you. I'm a very good sailor and the boat's hardly rolling at all.

SKRIBB (*raving*). T'cha ! Soldiers ! Rid our ruler of the rabble, and CLOSE THE GATES ! (*He exits furiously up L.*)

(OGBERT *and* EGBERT *come down with weapons to drive the* CROWD *off R. The* CROWD *retreat as they sing refrain* "And Shall we E'er be Paid," *etc. At the same time, a* SEA CAPTAIN, *down R., draws the* DAME *and* JOLIJAK *towards him to a corner.*

After the CROWD *have gone, followed by* OGBERT *and* EGBERT :—)

SEA CAPT. Now listen, Mother ! The Baron won't have your boy, but why not let him take a job with me, and come away to sea ?

DAME (*as they come C.*). Well, you are a nice sole. I suppose you're not codding ?

SEA CAPT. I'll make a fine sailor of him.

JOLIJAK. A sailor ! Oh, mother, let me go !

DAME. A sailor ? I must think it over.

SEA CAPT. No—he must come at once. My ship sails to-night.

DAME. Oh, all right. But promise he won't get drowned !

SEA CAPT. Drowned ? Ridiculous ! Can he swim ?

DAME. No, but he can sing.

SEA CAPT. Good ! It's sing or swim at sea, you know. Let's try him out. (*He sings* " Doh.")

DAME. We all sing at home. It's a family failing.

They go into :—
No. 4. TRIO. (DAME, JOLIJAK, CAPTAIN.)

(After Number—DANCE and exeunt down L.)

(The BARON enters up L., and strides down R.C., shouting " SKRIBB ! SKRIBB ! " SKRIBB follows him up L.)

SKRIBB.   Yes, my lord ?

BARON.   Has that woman gone ?

SKRIBB.   They have all gone. The gates are barred.

BARON.   What a distraction ! Just when I'm so worried.

SKRIBB.   Are you still worried ?

BARON.   Still worried—yes. What is more, I am distraught. That messenger who came to-day—where is he ?

SKRIBB.   Still in the dungeon.

BARON.   Keep him there. He brought bad news.

SKRIBB.   Bad news ?

BARON.   Yes—very bad. To-day my brother's family will descend upon this castle.

SKRIBB.   His family ? Descend on the Castle ?

BARON.   Yes—what does that mean ?

SKRIBB.   It means they're coming here.

BARON.   Fool ! Of course it does ! But I have not seen my brother for scores of years—he was much older. I did not know he had a family.

SKRIBB.   Ah !

BARON.   How big—or how old ! It may be a regiment of full-grown men !

SKRIBB.   Ah !

BARON.   To fight—and capture this castle !

SKRIBB.   Ah !

BARON.   Don't keep on saying "Ah " !

SKRIBB.   Ah—I mean—Oh !

BARON.   What can I do ?

SKRIBB.   You can but wait !

(EGBERT and OGBERT run on L.)

EGBERT. Master !

OGBERT. There is something **approaching** !

BARON. Ah ! It is ! What is it ?

EGBERT. Well—we *think* it's a horse !

OGBERT. And there are people on its back !

BARON. People ?

SKRIBB. It can't be a very large family, then.

BARON. Silence ! (*To up L., looking off.*) It may be a very large horse !

(MUSIC STARTS. NOISE OF HORSE HOOFS.)

EGBERT (*retreating to R.*). They're coming nearer !

OGBERT (*following*). They're getting smaller !

(*They're both looking off L., with* SKRIBB.)

SKRIBB. Why—they're not people !

OGBERT. They are children !

SKRIBB. They're heading straight for the castle !

BARON (*to C.*). Children ! Can it be—the first of my brother's family ?

OGBERT. Well—they may be the first—but the horse—my word—I'll bet he's never given the bookies a weak heart.

EGBERT. Here they come !

BARON. Yes ! Raise the gates and let them in!

(EGBERT *and* OGBERT *rush off up L. The* BARON *strides down R. to* SKRIBB.)

BARON. Children ! That means trouble !

SKRIBB. Aha ! We'll be a match for 'em !

(*The music has increased. Then a comic* HORSE *trots on down L., with* DIB *and* DOLLY *on its back, and* EGBERT *and* OGBERT *following, scared.*

The HORSE *circles the stage, and finally stops up L.C.* DIB *and* DOLLY *dismount and come to C.*)

BARON. Great Heavens ! (*To* OGBERT *and* EGBERT) Why didn't you stop the traffic ?

(OGBERT *and* EGBERT *gesticulate helplessly and make inarticulate sounds, then subside.*)

DIB (*to* BARON). Is this the Castle ?

DOLLY. Are you our Uncle ?

DIB. How dare you speak to him without an
    introduction ?
    Have you forgotten everything I told you of
    instruction ?
    (*To the* BARON).
    If you're the Baron Hugo, sir, I'm sure you
    will be glad to
    Know we have come here to stay, 'cos father
    said we had to.

BARON. One moment, boy ! Are you my nephew
      and is this my niece ?
      And has my brother sent you here that he
      may get some peace ?

DOLLY. Well, not exactly, for you see our father's
gone a journey,

DIB. Which may take years, and so meanwhile he's
made you his attorney.

DOLLY. He wants you to look after us—he says he
knows you'll do it.

DIB. And as we are quite well off, you certainly
won't rue it.

BARON. You're quite well off ? (*chuckling indul-
gently*). My dearest children ! Is that really so ?
You mean—you're rich ? But surely you are far too
    young to know ?

SKRIBB. Ah-HA !

BARON (*aside*). Shut up !

DOLLY. He told us so. And if we didn't live as long
    as you,
The wealth that now belongs to us would come along
    to you.

(BARON *and* SKRIBB *roar with laughter, clap each other
on the back, etc. Bus.*)

BARON (*after pushing* SKRIBB *away*). Ridiculous !
I'm charmed to have you here, my pretty namesake
Don't let us talk of things like that—forget them, do—
    for shame's sake.

DIB. Oh—Uncle—are you glad we came ?

BARON. If not, I'd be a sinner.

DOLLY. Dear Uncle Hugo—charming name !

BARON. Well, take 'em in to dinner !

BABES (*together, ad. lib.*). Oh, lovely, lovely ! We are so hungry !

(OGBERT *and* EGBERT *bow and scrape and usher the* BABES *off up* L. BARON *turns down* R.C. *to* SKRIBB.)

HORSE (*up C.*). Did you say dinner ?

BARON (*to* SKRIBB). Yes, for them, not for you.

SKRIBB. I didn't say anything.

HORSE. No, he didn't say anything.

BARON. There's an awful echo in this place. But about these children. Did you hear ?

SKRIBB. I heard, master. They are rich—they are helpless—and if they should . . .

BARON. Sh . . . sh !

SKRIBB. Then all their wealth will come to *you* !

BARON. Aha ! Skribb, have you an appetite for crime ?

HORSE. Did you say appetite ?

BARON (*to* SKRIBB). I did say appetite—don't keep repeating ! Now ! Get a load of . . . HEY !

(*The* HORSE *has come down and poked his head between them.*)

HORSE. Did you say " hay," sir ? I don't mind if I do !

(BARON *and* SKRIBB *stagger back with shouts of alarm, and calling* OGBERT *and* EGBERT. *The retainers rush in, followed by the* BABES.)

BARON. Ten thousand furies ! Take this animal away ! He talks too much !

(MUSIC. OGBERT *and* EGBERT *try to take the* HORSE *away. They get bitten.* BARON *and* SKRIBB *are kicked* R. *and* L. *The* HORSE *dances, to the* BABES' *delight. Finally they entice the* HORSE *off* L., *with cake.* BARON *and* SKRIBB *are left supporting each other at* R.C. OGBERT *and* EGBERT *ditto at* L.C. *Both couples puffing and blowing and hugging each other for protection as the* TABS CLOSE.)

END OF SCENE 1.

Act One. Scene 2.

Scene.—*On the way to the Wood.* (*Cut cloth, opening C., with a stile, and backing.*

(Egbert *marches on* L., *doggedly.*)

Egbert. Left, right, left, right, left, right . . . now then, come along, step it out, it can't be much further. . . . (*He looks round and finds that he is alone. Calling :*) Here, come along! And leave those blackberries alone!

(*Enter* Ogbert, *weary, at* L.)

Ogbert. It's all very well, but I've had about enough of this.

Egbert. Oh, you have, have you? Call yourself a soldier! I've a good mind to give you socks!

Ogbert. I wish you would. I've a hole in both heels.

Egbert. Courage, brother! The end is in sight!

Ogbert. That's what I said when I saw my heels.

Egbert. Oh, leave your heels alone! (*looking through the gap C.*) Can you see the sky-line?

Ogbert (*following to C.*) The what-line?

Egbert. The skyline—there, with the trees growing on it.

Ogbert. Oh—that!

Egbert. Yes, that! And that's the Forest!

Ogbert. You mean the Forest, *where* . . . ? (*Much moved.*) Oh, Egbert, I can't bear to think of it! Those two poor Babes!

Egbert. Don't be so soft! All we have to do is to lose them! (*suddenly affected by* Ogbert's *grief*). Oooh, it does seem so sad!

(*They weep on each other's shoulders.*)

Ogbert. They're so lovely!
Egbert. So docile.

OGBERT. So what ?

EGBERT. Docile.

OGBERT. I don't know what it means, but it sounds beyutiful !

EGBERT. The way they always wash behind their ears—it's pathetic !

OGBERT. To hear them gargle every night at bed-time—it's a most moving performance !

EGBERT. And now we have to get rid of them for ever !

(*They weep unrestrainedly, then suddenly recover and turn L., as* DIB *and* DOLLY *enter L., eating blackberries.*)

DOLLY. Oggy, darling, these are lovely !

DIB. I've got a capful !—do have some !

DOLLY. How kind you are to bring us to such a beautiful spot.

EGBERT (*sniffing*). I beg your pardon ?

OGBERT (*sniffing*). What was that ?

DOLLY. I said, how kind of you to bring us to such a . . .

EGBERT. Yes-yes-yes ! Don't mention it ! (*He blows his nose.*)

OGBERT. It's a pleasure ! (*gulps.*)

DIB. I say ! Will Uncle always let you come with us like this ?

EGBERT. I beg your pardon ?

OGBERT. Wassat ?

DIB. I say, will Uncle always let you come with us . . .

(OGBERT *and* EGBERT *almost begin a sob, then check themselves.*)

DOLLY. But you don't seem very happy, do you ? Shall we sing to you, to cheer you up ?

EGBERT *and* OGBERT (*together*). Thanks very much. We'd love a good laugh ! (*Bus.*) And just for the sake of argument, we'll join you.

They go into :—

No. 5.   QUARTETTE *and* DANCE (DOLLY *and* DIB,
                                OGBERT *and* EGBERT)

After Number :—

EGBERT.   That was very . . .

OGBERT.   Very . . .

EGBERT.   Very . . .

BOTH.   Nice. (*They bow.*)   At least—*we* were good.

DOLLY.   Well, where do we go now ?

DIB.   I'm fearfully hungry.   We'd better go home !

EGBERT.   I beg your pardon ?

OGBERT.   What was that ? (*They look at each other and gulp.*)

DOLLY (*to* DIB).   You know, I don't think they can hear very well !   (*To* EGBERT).   Can't we find something to eat besides blackberries ?

EGBERT.   Of course !   Of course !   I've got a picnic here !

(*He takes a packet of sandwiches out of his pouch.*)

DIB *and* DOLLY (*together*).   Oh !   What's that ?

EGBERT.   Sandwiches !   You'd better get over into the field and eat them.

DIB.   Sandwiches !

DOLLY.   Oh—that's splendid !

(*They climb over the stile C., and disappear.*)

OGBERT.   What d'you want to do that for ?   That's *our* rations !

EGBERT.   I k-k-know, b-b-but when I come to face it, I simply can't face it.

OGBERT.   What d'you mean ?   Orders, ain't it ?

EGBERT.   That's all very well.

OGBERT.   What did the Baron tell us ?   " Take 'em out into the wood and—get rid of 'em ! "

EGBERT.   Oh—shut up !

(NOISE *of* BIRDS *heard.*)

OGBERT.   Lor !—what's that ?

(*They both look over the stile.*)

EGBERT *and* OGBERT (*turning back from the stile, shielding their eyes*). Oh! Oh!

EGBERT. Look at it! What a sight! The last meal they may ever have!

OGBERT. Yes—and *that's* ours!

EGBERT. And they're feeding the birds with it!

OGBERT. Yus—with our rations!

EGBERT. Pah! Ain't you got any poetry inside you?

OGBERT. No—nor yet any sandwiches!

EGBERT. That's done it. I dissolve the partnership. You go and get rid of those two pretty innocents yourself.

OGBERT. I'll show you. (*He goes to the stile, looks over it, and comes back weeping.*) There's the prettiest little robin—

EGBERT. What did I tell you—

OGBERT. —eating *my* sandwiches!

EGBERT. Yah! You can't do it any more than I can!

OGBERT. Who can't?

EGBERT. You can't!

OGBERT. Who says I can't?

EGBERT. I says you can't!

OGBERT. Oh—you do, do you?

EGBERT. Yes—I do, do I!

OGBERT. I've a good mind to give you a real hard knock!

EGBERT. Oh—have you? (*He removes his waistcoat.*)

OGBERT. Yes.

EGBERT. Come on, then! (*He removes his waistcoat.*)

OGBERT. Yes—I think I shall.

EGBERT. You'd better. (*He removes another waistcoat.*)

OGBERT. Yes—I think I had.

EGBERT. One moment. (*He removes his remaining waistcoats.*)

OGBERT. What do you mean?

EGBERT. We'll do this thing properly, my boy.

MUSIC. (*He takes two top posts from stile, and plants them on stage. Takes rope from round his waist, fastens it to stile and to two posts, forming a boxing ring.* NOTE. *This bus. is not essential.*)

Now then—come on !

(*Burlesque boxing bout to hornpipe music. This is done as a short Boxing Ballet. They retire at end of each round to opposite corners and fan themselves. Finish with a double knock-out. They each count while lying on ground* " Two, four, six, eight, *ten !* " *and then lie still.*)

(DIB *and* DOLLY *appear at the stile. They come over and see the two on the ground. They shriek and rush off.*

(*B.O.* TABS CLOSE.)

During Scene change :

MUSIC, *or eccentric comedy dance by* OGBERT *and* EGBERT *in front of tabs.*)

END OF SCENE **2.**

ACT ONE.　SCENE 3.

SCENE.—*Deep in the Wood. There are entrances R.
and L., and up C.*

*Sunset lighting. There is soft MUSIC, and then a
number of children dressed as rabbits dance on at R.
and L. This should be spot-lit and a flicker wheel will
add to the effect.*

*Suddenly, the RABBITS stop, dead still. A crash of
music, B.O., and the RABBITS scurry off. The lighting
goes up again immediately and DIB and DOLLY are
on stage.*

DOLLY.　Oh—have we run far enough?

DIB.　I have—I'm winded!

DOLLY.　Oh, Dib—what were those dreadful men
doing?

DIB.　Fighting.

DOLLY.　And they'd killed each other! How
terrible!

DIB.　Well—we didn't stop to see if they had. I've
been wondering whether we ought to go back and see.

DOLLY.　Oh—no! I couldn't! Let's go home, Dib
dear.

DIB.　Yes—perhaps we'd better—or Uncle Hugo will
be angry.

DOLLY.　Yes—oh, yes! Which is the way?

DIB.　Well—here's a path (*they go up R.*).

(SPIDER'S WEB *rises R. and bars their path.*)
B

DOLLY. Oh, no! Look! A horrid spider's web!

DIB. Well, then—let's come this way. (*They go to L.*)

(BRAMBLES *rise and wave across the L. exit.*)

DOLLY. Oh, no! See, there are brambles every-where!

DIB. Then—here! (*They run to down R.*)

DOLLY. Don't! Don't! Not that way! It's nothing but thistles!

(*An enormous thistle walks on and bars the path down R.*)

DIB. But there must be *some* way!

(*They run about stage.*)

DOLLY. Dib! Dib! Don't let go my hand! I'm frightened! Where are we?

DIB. Don't be frightened, sister dear. We're only in the Wood.

DOLLY. Don't leave me, Dib dear. (*She sits on the bank up R.C.*) It's getting dark—and I'm getting cold. And I'm—frightened.

DIB. Ah—that's because you're tired. Don't worry, Dolly dear. I won't leave you—and (*boldly*) *I'm* not frightened.

They go into

No. 6.   DUET   ..   (DIB *and* DOLLY.)

(*After Number*, OWL HOOTS. *The lighting continues to fade.*)

DOLLY. Oh—what was that?

DIB. Er—er—an owl—that's all!

DOLLY. W-w-what d-did you s-say—about being frightened?

DIB. I s-s-said I-I-I'm not f-frightened!

DOLLY. Dib dear—it's getting dark!

DIB. Let it!

DOLLY. Isn't it cold?

DIB. I'm not cold. Here—take my cloak. (*He puts his cloak round her.*) We'll sit down for a while and rest. I'll take you home when you're not so tired. (*He sits by her side.*)

DOLLY. Oh, Dib dear—how clever you are. (DIB *puts his arms round her.*) Oh—how sleepy I am (*beginning to sleep*). Yes—we'll go home—you're so—clever. (*She sleeps.*)

DIB. I wish I were as clever as you think.

(*The owl hoots again.*)

Ugh! Yes—it *is* cold! I mustn't go to sleep! No! But I *should* like to! Dolly! Dolly! Oh—she *is* asleep! Ugh! I wonder if she could spare a corner of that cloak. Just a corner.

(*He lies down beside her and draws the corner of the cloak over himself.*) *I* won't go to sleep! (*But he does.*)

(*There is a tinkle of little bells, and then the* FAIRY OF GOOD INTENT *appears in the opening C., in a spot of light. She addresses the sleeping* BABES.)

FAIRY. Sleep sweetly, gentle babes, you're just
      beginning
      The tale of young folk sinned against—not
      sinning.
      Naught come between you and your happy
      dreaming
      Though far away the evil Baron's scheming.
      Dame Nature recalls your kindness to her
      feathered friends,
      You fed the robins—now she more robins
      sends.
      Kindness with kindness will be paid—you
      gave
      Your crumbs of bread. Now, they your lives
      will save.
      To hide you from your foes, protect you
      from the cold,

Make you a coverlet of autumn leaves, all
    green and gold.
When morning breaks, who knows what may
    be done
To herald in new fortune with the rising sun?

(*The* FAIRY *vanishes. A number of robins dance in, to
very soft music. They dance a* BALLET *of* ROBINS,
covering the BABES *with leaves, and exeunt.*)

No. 7. BALLET.

The distant song of birds, and hoot of owls as the TABS
CLOSE.

During Scene Change :

    Introduce DANCE OF ROBINS, *reprise in front of tabs,
with a Song and Refrain.*

END OF SCENE 3.

Act One.   Scene 4.

SCENE.—*The* Baron's *Study.*   (*Front inset scene.*)

(*The* Baron *is seated C., at a table.*

A clock, off stage, chimes Six.)

Baron.   The hour has struck ! By now the deed is done,
     No more those prattling babes shall ride a pillion,
     And I shall now inherit what I've won.
     I guess I shall be worth close on a million !
(*shouting*) Skribb !

(Skribb *enters L., carrying a parchment.*)

Skribb.   My lord ! You called ?

Baron.   Of course I did ! Have you run through that list of my young relatives' possessions ?

Skribb.   I should like to run through it, my lord—for it makes a mighty sum.

Baron.   Excellent ! Skribb—you've made a joke ! Ah ! It is a goodly sum—eh ?

Skribb.   An excellent sum. There's much more addition than subtraction about it.

Baron.   Ere we have finished, there shall be multiplication too !

Skribb (*holding out his hand, and grinning*). Yes, master, and what about a little *division*, also ?

Baron.   Pah ! Your greed and avarice sicken me ! Where are those villainous retainers of mine ? They are late !

Skribb (*slyly*).   I trust nothing has happened to the Babes ! (*he laughs villainously*).

BARON. Ho—ho—ho ! (*He laughs.*) What could have happened, eh ?

SKRIBB. He—he—he ! Children are so easily lost !

BARON. I should be most upset . . .

(BARON *and* SKRIBB *go into a fit of laughter, which is interrupted by a crash off L.*)

Aha ! My retainers ! I hear their gentle steps !

SKRIBB. Er—yes, my lord. It didn't sound like the *Babes* !

BARON. Ho—ho—ho ! I fear the worst ! Send those two cut-throats to me here ! I fear the worst, but I must worst my fear !

(SKRIBB *exits L., cackling with laughter.*)

What news have these brave fellows now, I wonder ? Am I indeed at last in reach of plunder ?

(OGBERT *and* EGBERT *stagger in wearily. Both have black eyes and much sticking plaster.*)

Ho ! My courageous henchmen ! (*sees their condition*) Great Missenden in Bucks ! What's this ?

EGBERT (*weakly*). We come, my lord.

OGBERT (*ditto*). As you commanded.

BARON. Well, brighten up, brighten up ! Have you done my bidding ?

EGBERT (*to* OGBERT). Have we done his bidding ! I ask you !

OGBERT.   Don't we look like it ?

BARON. Do you mean to tell me—

EGBERT (*points to plaster*). Blood speaks louder than words.

OGBERT. Oh, dear. Many willing hands make a headache.

BARON. Did they—struggle ?

EGBERT. We wrestled for hours—

OGBERT. But remembered our duty—

EGBERT. Come back alone, was your orders—

OGBERT. So we came back together.

BARON. Peace, fools—

EGBERT. Shut up, can't you ? He's talking to you.

BARON. Where are the Babes ?

EGBERT. A-ah ! Where *are* they ?

BARON. What do you mean, varlet ?

EGBERT. Well—if we're like *this*—

OGBERT. And we *won*, mind you—

EGBERT. What do you think *they* look like ?

BARON. I am well content. Go—you may have
your supper.

(*Instant rush of* EGBERT *and* OGBERT *towards the exit L.*)

Stay ! Stay !

(*They both pause.*)

OGBERT *and* EGBERT. Eh ?

BARON. You have done well. But—not a word !

OGBERT. Not even to the wife !

(*They creep off L. on tip-toe.*)

BARON. My schemes succeed ! The money now is
mine !

(*Enter* SKRIBB *L., very agitated.*)

SKRIBB. My lord ! My lord !

BARON. What is it *now* ?

SKRIBB. Oh, my master ! I have gone further into
this manuscript and have discovered a small clause !

BARON. Small clause ? Well, what about it ?

SKRIBB. Oh sir ! This small clause will tear your
scheme to ribbons ?

BARON. What !

SKRIBB. You are to inherit all this wealth—

BARON. Yes—yes—I know—

SKRIBB. But only if the Babes live—

BARON. *Live* ? Only if they LIVE ?

SKRIBB. Yes. Only if they live to the age of 20
years.

BARON. What ? There must be some mistake !

SKRIBB. Not in this manuscript, my lord.
BARON. Quick ! Call those men back !

(SKRIBB *runs off L.*)

What's this ? I thought that wealth for me their end
    meant.
Am I to be ruined by an amendment ?

(EGBERT *and* OGBERT *enter L., with sausages and mugs.*)

EGBERT. You don't want to cancel the supper ?
OGBERT. We'd just started !
BARON. Listen ! Did you *kill* the Babes ?
EGBERT. I beg your pardon ?
OGBERT. We don't quite get you !
BARON. Are they still alive ?
EGBERT. Did you wish them to live ?
OGBERT. Didn't you say—
BARON. Silence ! Did you kill the Babes ?
EGBERT. Well—if you put it like *that*—
OGBERT. Of course—speaking as man to baron—
BARON. Oh—we shall never get on like this. Listen !
I have decided that I shall be pleased if they are still
alive.
EGBERT. What ?
BARON. Alive—and well.
OGBERT. Oh—I say—that's a bit of a volty-facey !
BARON. Are—they—alive ?
EGBERT. Hum. Well—as a matter of fact—
BARON. Speak—knaves—*speak* !
OGBERT. All right then ! Tell the truth.
EGBERT. And shame the Baron !
BARON. *Are they* ALIVE ?
OGBERT. Well—er—yes !
BARON. They are ! They live !
EGBERT. They live ! They are !
BARON. Where are they ?
EGBERT *and* OGBERT (*together*). Eh ?
BARON. Did you lay hands on them ?
EGBERT *and* OGBERT (*together*). Oh—*no* !
BARON. Did they lay hands on you ?

EGBERT *and* OGBERT (*together*).   Oh—*no*!

BARON.   Then—what is the meaning of all this?

(*He points to their damaged faces.*)

EGBERT.   Oh—that was a little mutual argument . . .

OGBERT.   . . during which the Babes escaped.

BARON.   Escaped?

EGBERT.   Yes—like that.   Whish!   (*He waves his arm wildly and knocks* OGBERT *backwards*.)

OGBERT.   Yes—just like that—whish!   (*He also waves his arm wildly.* EGBERT *ducks, and* OGBERT *spins round and round.*)

BARON.   This is splendid!   Brave fellows!

EGBERT *and* OGBERT (*together*).   What?   (*they look behind them*).

OGBERT.   It's all right—don't look round—he means us.

BARON.   Go and find two suppers—then go and find the Babes!

EGBERT.   What?

OGBERT (*aside, digging* EGBERT *in the ribs*).   Shut up! Go and find two suppers—then go and find the Babes!

(*They rush off L.*)

BARON. All is not lost that shivers!   The end is in
         sight!
       We'll find the Babes and they shall live to 20
         years!
       Yes—live safely!   In my dungeon!   Till 20
         years!
       And not a minute more!   Ha!   Ha!   Ha!

(BLACK-OUT.   TABS CLOSE.)

MUSIC *during* SCENE CHANGE.

END OF SCENE 4.

ACT ONE.   SCENE 5.

SCENE.—*Deep in the Wood.* (*As in Scene* 3.)

As the curtain rises, there is music, and the lighting comes up slowly to full.

The BABES *are still asleep under their canopy of leaves. Off stage, a cock crows.*

A short BALLET *of* BIRDS *and* RABBITS *might be introduced at this point. After this,* TWO SQUIRRELS *enter.—(If practicable, down a tree.)*

1ST SQUIRREL (*after a few steps to music*).
   A lovely morning, wifie dear,
   Perhaps a trifle chilly.
2nd SQUIRREL. I'll need a new fur coat this year.
1ST SQUIRREL. Now darling, don't be silly !
   We'll talk of that at Christmas, pet,
   I'm worried . . .
2nd SQUIRREL.   What's the reason ?
1ST SQUIRREL.   There's nothing in our larder yet
   And nuts are now in season.

A shower of nuts falls from above.   As they gather nuts :)

2nd SQUIRREL. I'm sure I do my best all day
   At cooking and house-keeping . . .

(1st SQUIRREL *turns over leaves and reveals the* BABES.)

1ST SQUIRREL. Good Heavens, darling ! Let's away !
   Two giants there—a-sleeping !

(*They scurry off squeaking loudly as* DIB *rises from the leaves.*)

DIB. Oh ! What was that ? (*He shakes* DOLLY.) Dolly ! Dolly !
DOLLY (*coming up from under the leaves*). Why— wherever are we ?
DIB. In the forest !

DOLLY (*stretching and rubbing her eyes*). Of course ! In the forest ! I've been dreaming. I dreamed I was running away from someone.

DIB. I've been dreaming, too. It must have been a long dream—look ! We're covered with leaves ! We must have been asleep for hours !

DOLLY. What's the time, I wonder ?

DIB. Breakfast time, I hope. I'm ever so hungry.

DOLLY. But where's the breakfast ?

(DIB *rises and crosses L.C.*)

DIB. Don't ask questions like that—I'm thinking.

DOLLY (*rising and coming to C.*). But isn't there any breakfast ?

DIB. How would you like—say, some mushrooms, blackberries, a new-laid egg, and some hazel nuts ?

DOLLY. Oh, Dib, how clever you are ! Let's sit down and have it now !

DIB. Now isn't that like a woman ! I said " How would you like it ? " We've got to find it first.

DOLLY. Oh. Yes, of course. We must go home . . . Dib !

DIB. Yes. Exactly. We're lost, you know.

DOLLY. Lost !

DIB. And we've got to look after ourselves now. Oh, Dolly, what are we going to do ?

DOLLY. Well, if we can't have breakfast we can have a song. It may give us ideas.

DIB. What—for breakfast ?

DOLLY. No, silly. For finding our way.

They go into :—

No. 8.   *Duet (Reprise of No. 6)* (DOLLY *and* DIB)

After Number :—

DOLLY. How do you feel now ?

DIB. Hungrier than ever . . . (*He sees two or three large mushrooms rise from the ground*) . . . oh, Dolly ! Look ! Mushrooms !

DOLLY. Lovely ! Let's make a start ! (*They pick up two mushrooms.*)

DIB.   If only we had a frying pan !

DOLLY.   And a fire !

DIB.   And a little bit of butter !

DOLLY.   And a rasher of bacon . . .

(*A loud sizzling noise is heard.*)

DIB.   What's that ?

DOLLY.   Dib ! It is ! It is !

DIB.   Is what ?

DOLLY.   Can't you smell it ? Someone—frying—
BACON !

(*A siren sounds in the distance.*)

CHILDREN (*off R.*)   Breakfast ! Breakfast !

(*The* BABES *retreat up L.C., as the* CHILDREN *of* DAME
TRUFORM, *headed by* BLAKEY, *a boy, and* CHERRY-
BLOSSOM, *a girl, enter R.*)

(NOTE : LILLI *and* SKINNA *are not in this scene.*)

CHILDREN (*running on*).   Hurrah for breakfast !

(*They check on seeing the* BABES.)
OH !

DIB (*politely*).   Good morning.

BLAKEY.   Good morning. Who are you ?

DIB.   Well, I'm Dib, and this is my sister Dolly.

DOLLY.   Good morning. Er—whom have we the
pleasure of . . .

CHILDREN (*grouping around the* BABES).   Don't you
know who *we* are ?

DOLLY.   I'm afraid we don't.

DIB.   Not the least idea.

(*A chorus of cries of astonishment.*)

BLAKEY.   We're the children of the Little Old
Woman . . .

CHERRY.   Who lived in a Shoe !

DIB.   Oh yes ! She had so many children she didn't
know what to do. I remember now.

DOLLY.   That's right—she didn't know what to do.

CHERRY. That's what the story books say, but wait till you've met Mother ! By the way, have you had breakfast ?

DOLLY. Well—er—we had breakfast *yesterday*— rather early—and rather a small one.

BLAKEY. A big lunch perhaps ?

DIB. No, j-just a s-s-snack.

CHERRY. Tea ?

DOLLY. We—er missed it.

DIB. We couldn't get back for supper . . .

DOLLY. In fact we're l-l-lost !

CHILDREN. Lost ! How LOVELY !

(DOLLY *and* DIB *look at each other.*)

CHERRY. Excuse me, but would you object to having breakfast with *us* ?

BLAKEY. Don't if you don't *care* to !

DOLLY *and* DIB (*together*). Care to ! Object ! O-oh ! We're starving !

CHERRY. Splendid ! Well, the first breakfast whistle's gone, so what about a song to keep us going till the bacon's fried ?

They go into :—

No. 9.   ENSEMBLE .. (*Song by* CHERRYBLOSSOM *and chorus of* CHILDREN.)

(*This Number should be of a very rousing character.*)

CURTAIN.

END OF ACT ONE.

ACT TWO.

SCENE 1.

SCENE.—DAME TRUFORM'S BOWER. (*See the* GROUND PLAN.)

The scene is backed by a sky-cloth. A low ground row of river bank and low hedge, with a gap C. In the gap, above the bank, is the SHOE, *which may be partially hidden by trees. It is fitted up as a house, into which characters may enter and disappear. There is a gangplank leading from the bank to the* SHOE. *Forest scenery all round, and entrances R. and L.*

A huge kettle on a tripod over a fire at up R.C.

When the CURTAIN *rises,* EIGHT CHILDREN *are dancing in a ring at down L.C., hands joined and chanting :—*

ALL. There was an old woman who lived in a shoe,
         Shoodle—oodle—oodly—oo,
         With children who numbered much more than
            a few,
         Shoodle—oodle—oodly—oo.
         With her and her husband,
         They numbered three dozen,
         In all kinds of weather,
         There's nothing like leather.
         To live in this new form,
         Just suited Dame Truform,
         Shoodle—oodle—oodly—oo.
         Shoodle—oodle—oodly—oo.

(*Enter* DAME TRUFORM *from the shoe, carrying a large frying-pan.*)

DAME. How many times have I told you that I *will* not have singing before breakfast ? All this running up and down your scales gives you too much of an appetite —besides, it wears your boots out.

CHILD (*creeping up to her*). But, Ma—

DAME. Now then—take your fingers off the bacon, can't you? What do you think this is—a cafeteria? (*counts*) 1—2—3—4—5—6—7—8—where are the rest of you?

2nd CHILD. They're coming along with two children we found.

DAME. Two children? Two more? What did you want to go and find them for?

3rd CHILD. We couldn't help it—they were lost. They're coming to breakfast with us!

DAME. Oh, are they? Thanks for telling me. If this goes on we shall have to take the shoe next door—when it's been soled and heeled. (*Shouting*) Lilli! LILLI!

(LILLI *enters from the Shoe.*)

LILLI (*shouting*). Yes Ma!

DAME. Don't shout like that!

LILLI. Well, you shouted.

DAME. I know I did. I'm the big noise round here. Where's your sister Skinna? Where are the twins, Nugget and Kiwi?

LILLI. Polishing the Toe-Cap.

DAME. Yes, and forgetting the back of the Heel, as usual, I suppose. Where's your father?

LILLI. Just gone to sleep.

DAME. Gone to sleep, has he? Sound the blower, my dear—at once. We shall never get breakfast done.

(LILLI *holds the siren to the kettle spout, steam comes out, and the siren sounds.* SKINNA, NUGGET *and* KIWI *enter from the Shoe.*)

ALL. Breakfast! Breakfast! Hurrah! Hurrah!

DAME. Come along! Get yourselves sorted out!

(MUSIC. *The* CHILDREN *form up on either side.* SKINNA *appears at the door of the Shoe with trick pile of plates, which* LILLI *takes and* SKINNA *gets another pile. The trick plates shoot out into a long line in front of children.* LILLI *and* SKINNA *distribute rashers and put them on plates, while* DAME *cuts up trick loaf and flings slices to children.*)

DAME. Now—are we ready ? Remember your manners, children. On the word " go " seize the bacon firmly between the right finger and thumb, and with a smart upward movement, place it on the bread. Go !

(They all do this.)

Don't fumble with your food—slap it on the bread. And don't lean on the bacon, or you'll make it streaky.

(CLARENCE TRUFORM *appears at the Shoe door. In appearance he is exactly like Strube's Little Man.*)

Ah ! Oh—you have got down, then !

CLARENCE. No—my dear—I've just got *up.*

(LILLI *and* SKINNA *give him some breakfast. He sits on the gang-plank to eat it.* LILLI *and* SKINNA *go above the tripod and take some bacon, etc.*)

DAME. There's no need to be funny—in front of the family too—*and* visitors expected !

CLARENCE. Visitors, dear ?

DAME. Yes, we're going to have two more children —just bed and breakfast—let's hope they're not theatricals.

CLARENCE. They'd better have that little room above the Instep.

DAME. Why didn't we rent a wide-fitting Men's Wellington instead of a one-button narrow-fitting Size Three Ladies' ? Ah well ! It never rains but it pours !

She goes into :—

No. 10.   SONG   ..   (DAME TRUFORM)

(Refrain and Dance.)

(CHILDREN *join in the Refrain.*)

After Number :—

ALL. Oh—Ma—Look ! *(They point to R.)* Here they are !

DAME. Who ? Where ?

LILLI. Well, I never !

(DIB *and* DOLLY *enter L., hand in hand, with the other* CHILDREN.)

DAME. Hum—hikers ! (*To* CLARENCE.) **Go on—tell** them they're trespassing.

CLARENCE. What ?

DAME. Trespassing !

CLARENCE (*coughing and approaching the* BABES). Er—I suppose you're just passing ?

DIB. We're lost !

CLARENCE. Lost ?

DAME. Nonsense ! How can they be lost ? They're *here* !

CHERRY. But they are lost ! They want to know the way to the Castle !

DOLLY. Yes, please. Can you tell us the way to the Castle ?

CLARENCE. The Castle ?

DAME. Oh, don't ask him ! The only Castle he knows has an Elephant on it. The Castle, eh ? You must be noble !

DIB. I don't know. But we're very hungry.

DAME. Why—of course ! Just one moment, while I get you something, and you shall tell me all.

DOLLY. Is this all your family ?

DAME. All ? Isn't it enough ? What did you think it was—the Primrose League ? Yes—here they are— here are Freeman—Hardy—and Willis—three little imps of mischief—and this is Lotus—and this is Saxone. I call him Saxone, because he's always So-rosis. And here are Day and Martin. This is Cherryblossom, and this is little Nugget—he's a glacé kid, I can tell you. And these are my eldest—Lilli and (*shouts*) LIL-LI !

LILLI (*behind the tripod, shouting*). Yes—Ma !

DAME. Don't shout ! Where's your sister Skinna ?

SKINNA (*who has been hiding behind* LILLI). Here, Ma !

DAME. Ah, yes—my twins—Lilli and Skinna Now run along—the pair of you—and help your pa wash up.

CLARENCE. Help me—

DAME. Wash up, I said.

CLARENCE. But I haven't finished my bacon.

DAME. Never mind—you can use that to dry the plates with.

(CLARENCE *and all the* TRUFORM CHILDREN *go into the Shoe.*)

DIB. Oh, please—

DOLLY. Yes—that's what I was going to say.

DIB. If we give you this mushroom, can we stay with you ?

DAME. Well—I don't know that we've got much room for *you.* However—a mother's heart—well, anyway, there's still a little bacon.

(*She takes an elastic rasher from the frying-pan.*)

Hum. Only one left. Still—that's the best of prime Wiltshire—it goes much farther.

(*The* BABES *take the ends of the rasher and pull it out to a great length and* DAME *cuts it in the middle.*)

DIB. Oh—thank you.

DOLLY. Er—thank you.

DAME. And how did you pretty dears get lost ?

DIB. Well—our Uncle Hugo—Baron Hugo . . .

DAME. What—the *Baron* ?

DOLLY. You know him ?

DAME. Well—not to say *know* exactly.

DIB. He sent us out for a walk with two *dreadful* men.

DAME. Yes—he *would.*

DOLLY. And the men fought.

DIB. We ran away—

DOLLY. And got lost.

DIB (*turning to face L.*). Oh—look ! Here they come !

DOLLY. Oh—save us ! Save us !

(*Both* BABES *clutch* DAME TRUFORM's *skirts.*)

DAME. Hush ! (*She pushes them up L.C.*) Bend down!

(*The* BABES *bend down,* DAME *throws a tablecloth over them and makes them look like a table.*)

And listen ! This is going to be good !

(*Enter* EGBERT *and* OGBERT, *examining the ground through magnifying glasses.*)

EGBERT. Lor! There's thousands of footprints here!

DAME. And why not indeed?

(EGBERT, *seeing* DAME TRUFORM, *comes to a dead stop and* OGBERT *runs into his back.*)

EGBERT. Ah! A woman!

OGBERT. My word—what a peach!

DAME. I wish I could say the same of you. But you look like a rotten "pair" to me.

EGBERT. We've no time for trifling.

DAME. It would take you some time to find someone to trifle with—with a face like that.

OGBERT. You're in no danger, anyhow.

EGBERT. Woman—have you seen two children?

DAME (*scornfully*). Have I seen two children? (*shouts*) Lil-li!

LILLI (*running out of the Shoe and shouting*). Yes—Ma!

DAME. Ah! Don't spatter me like that! Take the family out for a walk.

(MUSIC. *The* CHILDREN *run out of the Shoe, across and exeunt R.*)

EGBERT (*creeping down R., and watching the* CHILDREN *off*). Lumme—what was that?

OGBERT (*who has followed him*). That's a family—that was.

(*While they are watching the* CHILDREN *go, the* DAME *smuggles* DIB *and* DOLLY *up into the Shoe, and then comes down, shaking out tablecloth.*)

DAME. Yes, sir—that's my family. Have you anything to say?

EGBERT (*turning at R.*). Er—no.

OGBERT. No—I think we'd better not. (*They exchange glances.*)

(CLARENCE *appears at the door of the Shoe drying plates.*)

DAME. And here's their father. And he'll stand no impertinence, I can tell you. Clarence dear—come here.

CLARENCE. Yes, my dear (*coming down L.C.*). Who are these gentlemen ?

DAME (*at C.*). Gentlemen ? Oh—you must excuse him—he's shortsighted. They're looking for two children.

CLARENCE. Is that all they want ? Because, if so—

DAME. That'll do, dear. You haven't seen two strange children, have you ? (*aside*) Say " No," can't you ?

CLARENCE (*dropping a plate*). Er—

DAME. What did you say ?

CLARENCE. Er—no—my dear.

DAME. There you are, you see ! You'll say something else in a minute, I can tell you—dropping my half-a-crown Derby like that.

EGBERT. It's most urgent.

OGBERT. They're wanted immediate, by the Baron.

DAME. I'm sorry I can't oblige. You've seen all of my family—all except the eldest—and he's gone for a sailor.

EGBERT. Gone for a sailor ? Why—

OGBERT. Of course. I thought your face seemed familiar.

DAME. Never you mind what my face seems like.

EGBERT. No—don't worry about it—it'll only make you feel worse.

DAME. I . . . ! (*To* CLARENCE.) And are you going to stand there and let two hulking great men talk to your poor little wife like that, you wretched worm ?

CLARENCE. No—er—yes.

DAME. I thought so. Well, it's no use quarrelling. (*To* OGBERT.) What were you about to say ?

OGBERT. Your boy—Jolijak—he got the job, did he ?

DAME. Yes—he went for a sailor and he's to get fourteen shillings a week. Funny—the only time I went for a sailor—with a flat-iron—I got thirty shillings or a month. Isn't life a scream ?

They go into :—

No. 11. QUARTETTE .. (DAME, CLARENCE, OGBERT, EGBERT)

EGBERT. Well—I suppose we shall have to go on scouring the forest.

OGBERT. Yes—they ain't here.

EGBERT. But the Baron will see red if we don't get them kids into his clutches again.

DAME. Indeed ? Speak on—you interest me.

OGBERT. We can't stop here.

EGBERT. No—we must get on.

OGBERT. Or get out.

EGBERT. Which way does this go ? (*pointing R.*)

DAME. Oh—this way ! (*pointing R.*)

EGBERT. And where does that way go ? (*pointing further up R.*)

DAME. Oh—if you keep straight on, you'll find you can't go crooked.

OGBERT. We will ! Come, brother !

EGBERT. We'll soon have them under lock and key !

(*They go off R.*)

CLARENCE. Oh—what a relief.

DAME. Hush ! There is danger afoot !

CLARENCE. Where ? (*He looks round.*)

DAME. I can smell it—so could you, if you had a nose, instead of a moustache hook. Clarence ! Those men mean no good. I should not have let them go. Oh—I blame myself ! I blame myself !

CLARENCE. There ! Come ! Come !

DAME. It isn't " Come, come "—it's " Go, go." ! Quick ! Fetch me that flask of buttercup wine !

CLARENCE. Buttercup wine, dear ?

DAME. Buttercup wine, I said ! Scram !

(CLARENCE *exits into the Shoe.*)

The plot begins, with mischief brewing,
And I, for one, must now be up and doing.
To save those Babes at once I really must
Do something all those villains' plans to bust!
I'll overtake 'em now and undertake to
    throttle
Their evil schemes—CLARENCE! Bring
    me that bottle!

(BLACK OUT.)

During Scene change :

   The CHILDREN *enter in front of tabs from R. and L.,
and going into a song refrain and dance.*

END OF SCENE 1.

Act TWO.   Scene 2.

Scene.—*On the way to the Wood.* (*As in Act* 1, *Scene* 2.)

(Ogbert *and* Egbert *climb over the stile C., and look off R. and L.*)

Egbert (*coming to C.*). They can't have come this way.

Ogbert. Why not ? *We* have.

Egbert. I'm not so sure ! I think we're on the wrong track.

Ogbert. Well—she said " Turn to the right " when we left her.

Egbert. Yes, if we'd left it at that we'd have been right.

Ogbert. I don't quite follow.

Egbert. When we went right we went wrong.

Ogbert. Then all that's left is to get right again.

Egbert. Then where shall we be ? (*He turns away L.*)

Ogbert. We shan't know, shall we ?

Egbert (*with a sudden shout*). A-AH !

Ogbert (*staggering*). I wish you wouldn't go off like that !

Egbert. Hush ! I see a maiden tripping through the glade.

Ogbert. Well, let her trip.

(*Crash off.*)

Egbert. She has !

(*The* Dame *makes a "head over heels" or tumbling entrance at L.*)

Ogbert. Ha ! 'Tis she !
Egbert. Tishy ?
Dame (*picking herself up*). Hullo, boys ! Still here ? I thought I'd just drop in. You've wandered a bit, haven't you ?

OGBERT. You have misled us . . . (*he advances on her menacingly*).

EGBERT. And we know why . . .

(*Ditto bus. as* OGBERT *gets round to* L. *of the* DAME.)

DAME. Ho! Look at 'em! Down in the forest something stirred!

OGBERT *and* EGBERT (*together*). Don't trifle with us! Where are the Babes?

DAME. Ah! You want the best Babes—we have them. Is that the idea?

EGBERT. She admits it!

OGBERT. She has confessed!

EGBERT *and* OGBERT. Where are the Babes?

DAME. I haven't the least idea! What a couple of dear darling worriers you boys are. You'll find them soon.

EGBERT. We shall!

OGBERT. We mean to!

DAME (*taking a bottle out of her bag*). In the meantime, what about a little drop of my buttercup wine? I'm taking this to a sick friend.

OGBERT. Is he very sick?

DAME. Not very. He hasn't had any of this yet. Well, here's fun! (*She drinks from the bottle.*)

EGBERT (*taking the bottle and drinking*). Same to you. (*He gives the bottle to the* DAME, *who hands it to* OGBERT.)

OGBERT (*after drinking*). Very pleasant . . .

EGBERT (*snatching the bottle and drinking*). Wonderful bouquet!

OGBERT (*same bus.*). Smooth as silk!

EGBERT (*same bus.*). Just like milk!

OGBERT (*same bus.*). Your friend won't get much better at this rate.

EGBERT (*same bus.*). Here's a health to him, anyway.

OGBERT (*same bus.*). Without medicine . . .

(*During the above, the* DAME *has watched the passage of the bottle from side to side and ends with patiently casting her eyes up and folding her hands.*)

EGBERT (*same bus.*). Med'cine ? 'Diculous !

OGBERT (*same bus.*). Fantastic !

DAME (*suddenly roused*). Hey ! This is where you come in ! (*She takes the bottle.*) You boys really must be getting on.

EGBERT (*putting an arm round her*). We're getting on splendidly !

OGBERT (*putting an arm round her.*) Beau'f'ly ! Lovely creature !

DAME. I said " getting on " not getting " off." (*She pushes them both towards R.*)

OGBERT. I don't remember what we came for.

EGBERT. I do—a nice cosy forty winks !

DAME. No—no ! Back to the Castle—and tell the Baron you can't find them !

OGBERT. Find who ?

DAME. Them !

EGBERT. Splendid ! Who are they ?

DAME. The Babes !

OGBERT. Of course ! We want the best Babes . . .

EGBERT. She has them !

(*They both go off into roars of laughter, slapping each other on the back, etc., then suddenly stop as if petrified, and then walk off together, like sleepwalkers.*)

DAME. No ! No ! It cannot be ! Or have I put my foot in it ?

(*She turns to the stile, and the FAIRY appears there.*)

Oh ! Good gracious ! If this is what buttercup wine does . . .

FAIRY. Fear not, Dame Truform ! Yet, be very wary !

DAME. Oh, goodness me—I've had affaires, but never seen a Fairy !

FAIRY. Your life and family are in some danger, do not doubt it.

DAME. That's very kind of you—what can I do about it ?

Fairy. Those men will tell the Baron they believe
the Babes now shelter
        Within your house . . .
Dame. . . . oh dear ! Then we'd best helter-
skelter !
Fairy. Yes, move your children—all the twenty-
three . . .
Dame. And my old man ?
Fairy. . . . Yes, take them all and sail right out
to sea !
Leave not a soul behind ! And take on board each
        living biped !
    Dame. We will ! I know my house will float —be-
    cause it's soled with Driped !

(Black Out.)

End of Scene 2.

(Music *to carry through to next scene.*)

Act TWO. Scene 3.

SCENE.—DAME TRUFORM'S BOWER. (*As in Scene* 1.)

(*When the curtain rises—or running tabs open—the children, including* DIB *and* DOLLY, *are dancing in a ring, singing a chorus, with* CLARENCE *in the centre, with a garland of flowers on his head.*)

No. 12. OPENING CHORUS .. (CLARENCE *and* CHILDREN)

After one refrain and dance, enter DAME TRUFORM *at R., upstage.*

DAME. STOP !

(*They all stop, and the ring breaks to form an open group.* CLARENCE *to down L.C.*)

(*coming to C.*) We're off !

CLARENCE. What do you mean, dear—off ?

DAME. We're off to sea ! At once ! Now ! Without delay !

(*Cries of delight from the* CHILDREN, *who dance about.*)

Quiet !

CLARENCE. But—why, dear ?

DAME. To escape from the Baron and those two dirty dogs he sent snooping round—and to save the Babes ! To save our guests—Dib and Dolly !

DIB. But are we in danger ?

DAME. Yes, but don't ask me to explain—I can only tell you what the Fairy told me !

(*All retreat rather frightened.*)

CLARENCE. Th-th-the F-f-f-fairy, d-d-dear ?

DAME. Yes, there are fairies at the bottom of our garden—didn't you know ?

CLARENCE. No, dear.

DAME. Well, you do now. So tie up the boot and make fast ere we sail away.

CLARENCE. But, if I tie it up we shan't make it fast—we shan't be able to move !

DAME. Tie up ! Make fast ! Do as I say ! We must pack and then weigh anchor ! Clarence, be off and do as I say . . .

(CLARENCE, *dithering, runs into the Shoe.*)

Children, go and pick some nuts and apples, gather eggs, milk the goat, brush your boots, wash your necks, and be back in two minutes . . .

(*All the children except* DIB *and* DOLLY *run off down R., laughing and shouting.*)

DIB.   How grand to sail a Shoe across the ocean
          Why you should be so kind we have no notion.
DOLLY. Dame Truform, are you really going to let it
          Take us to safety? We never shall forget it.
DAME. To spite your uncle I would sail the seven
          seas
          So hurry, dears, and mind the step on, please.
          I've never had adventures, but for you I'll
          try one.
          Kind hearts are more than cornets—stop me
          and buy one !

(*She hurries the* BABES *across the plank into the Shoe. They disappear.*)

Clarence ! CLARENCE !

(CLARENCE *appears from the Shoe.*)

CLARENCE.   Yes, my dear ?
DAME.   Have you made fast ?
CLARENCE.   I'm not quite sure, dear !
DAME.   Oh, what a man ! Have you tied it up ?
CLARENCE.   Oh yes, I've tidied up everything !
DAME.   Gr-r-r-r ! If only I had my Jolijak here, he's a sailor ! Where's the rope, man ! The rope !
CLARENCE.   Oh—the rope ! Here it is, dear !

(*He throws the rope and it hits her.*)

DAME. Clarence, I shall have a few words with you

later. In the meantime, we've no time to lose. Is she floating all right ?

CLARENCE. Oh, rather ! Right on top of the water !

DAME. Where did you think it would float—on the bottom of the river ? Then stand by ! I'll call the family aboard !

(*She goes and works the traffic lights on the post, down R.*)

All aboard ! All aboard ! ALL ABOARD !

CLARENCE (*shouting and waving his arms wildly*). ALL ABOARD !

(*He overbalances and clutches the punting pole.*)

BOTH (*together*). Stopping at Ramsgate, Moorgate, Liverpool Street, The Bank !

(MUSIC. *All the children run on at R., dancing and shouting. DAME TRUFORM hurries them across the plank, and they disappear. She counts them with gestures as they go in.*)

CLARENCE. Is that all, my dear ? (*He takes up the pole.*)

DAME. Huh ! You don't count me, you brute !

(*The BABES have appeared on the Shoe. The DAME unties the rope, and mounts the plank.*)

Now, haul on the rope, and one good push !

CLARENCE. And away we go !

(*He gives a push with the pole, and the DAME falls into the water.*)

DIB and DOLLY. Oh, quick ! Quick !

(*They stoop and pick up the DAME, hauling her into the Shoe.*)

DAME. Thank you, my dears. Would you mind going inside a moment ? I want to give my husband my kind regards.

CLARENCE. You can't touch me—I'm touching wood!

(*A hunting horn is heard faintly, off.*)

DIB. Hark ! What's that ?

Dolly. Our Uncle's hunting horn ! The hounds are out !

Dame. The hounds ! The dirty dogs are out !

(The other Children *are seen on the top of the Shoe, crowding excitedly.)*

Clarence. They're hunting us ! That's not my line of hunting !

Dame. Come—all together ! Do a spot of punting !

*(*Music. *The lights fade, except on the Shoe. Moonlight on sky-cloth, against which the Shoe and characters are silhouetted.*

*The Shoe begins to move slowly. (*Note : *If it cannot be made to float across, it should rock gently, and, if possible, draw away from the bank.)*

All *sing a refrain of a boating song and work with punt poles.*

No. 13. Boating Chorus .. Ensemble)

Crescendo singing, fade lighting, as the Tabs Close.

End of Scene 3,

During Scene Change :—

In front of tabs, introduce a " sinister " Quartette Number for Baron, Skribb, Ogbert *and* Egbert. *Alternatively, a song for a* Girl, *with chorus of* Bathing Girls. *The repeat refrain of this, if employed, may serve as opening number of the next scene, the girls dancing up into the scene as the tabs open.*

Act Two.   Scene 4.

Scene.—*The* Palm Beach *at* Berm-on-Sea.

> (*Sky-cloth, with rostrum below it, low rock ground row and rock and palm wings R. and L.*)

> *The scene opens with Bathing Girls on. They go into :—*

No. 14.   Opening Chorus   .. (Bathing Girls
                                          and Boys.)

> (*This may be followed by a " Bathing Ballet.*")

> *After the Number :—*
>   (*Enter* Dib *and* Dolly.)

Dib.   I say, you others, what a lovely spot,
            There's sun and sand and sea in each direc-
                tion.

Dolly. I'd no idea the sea could be so hot,
            I feel as if I'd roasted my complexion.

Dib.   Why—look ! Who comes ?

All.   It's Jolijak the Sailor !

Dolly.   Jolijak ?

Children.   Yes—Jolijak—our eldest brother !

(*Enter* Jolijak. *The* Children *swarm round him.*)

Dolly.   Dib ! What a handsome man !

Dib. Not bad. But you girls are all alike. One touch of sailor makes the best girl his.

Dolly. Don't be jealous. He *is* handsome.

Dib. Handsome is as handsome—

Dolly. You needn't worry. I learnt that the year, before you did. Anyway—Ahem !

Dib.   Dolly ! Don't be so forward !

Dolly.   Ahem !

Jolijak.   Why—who are these ? Young lady— what's your name ?

Dolly (*frigidly*). If you don't know my name, sir, you'd better not speak to me.

DIB. She's my sister, let me tell you !

JOLIJAK. Yes—but she can't help that. (*To the* CHILDREN). Introduce me, imps.

ALL. They are Dib and Dolly, from the Castle.

JOLIJAK. The Castle ? Oh ! (*He goes on his knee to* DOLLY.) I beg your pardon.

DOLLY. That's much better. (*She gives him her hand.*) How do you do ? Lovely weather for the weather, is it not ?

DIB. Oh, you women ! (*He stalks away R.*)

DOLLY. Dib, don't go ! (*She moves R.*)

(DIB *exits R.*)

JOLIJAK. No, don't go ! (DOLLY *checks and turns to him.*)

DOLLY. Why not ?

JOLIJAK. Well, it's so long since I met anyone like you. I've been away to sea.

DOLLY. Really ? So you're a sailor ?

They go into :—

No. 15. DUET .. (JOLIJAK *and* DOLLY, *and* CHORUS)

(*After Refrain and Dance, the* CHORUS *exeunt R.*)

JOLIJAK. I say—I hope you don't think I've said too much ?

DOLLY. I said some of it.

JOLIJAK. Why—where are the others ?

DOLLY. Oh—I expect they've gone to tell your mother that you've arrived.

JOLIJAK. Ah, yes—of course. (*He runs up the bank at the back.*) Yes—you're quite right ! Oh ! My word ! My mother !

(*The* CHORUS *run on at up R. and down R., singing the refrain of the " Bathing Chorus " (No. 14). They group around the stage as* DAME TRUFORM *makes a spectacular entrance up C., clad in a Victorian bathing costume. She is followed by* CLARENCE *in paddling outfit, spade and pail.* DIB *has also re-entered with* LILLI *and* SKINNA.)

JOLIJAK (*dramatically*). She comes! My mother!

DAME. He's here! My-son-my-son-my-son!

(*They embrace fervently.*)

Oh, doesn't he look marvellous! You'd hardly know him from Clark Gable! (*Turning to* CLARENCE.) And to think he's *your* son! Wonders will never cease!

JOLIJAK. Ma! This is flattery!

DAME. Well, it's not my fault, dearie. If I can't get flatter, I must go in for flattery. But how are you —are you doing well?

JOLIJAK. Yes—very well.

DAME. They don't make you sleep on the haddocks, do they, dearie? Such nasty damp things, but I'm told that's how they get them so flat.

JOLIJAK. But what are you doing here?

DAME. Oh—just a little cruise, dear. Your father insisted on it.

CLARENCE. I—

DAME. Oh—do stop chattering, Clarence.

JOLIJAK. And you sailed the old home down here?

DAME. Oh, yes—we had a lovely sail—everything down to ninety-three and fourpence. Your father—

CLARENCE. And all the —

DAME. Interrupting you for one moment, if you please.

JOLIJAK. Did you find it easy?

DAME. Oh, yes. A boot's quite easy to sail. You can always get a tow—and you never heel over.

JOLIJAK. Well, Ma—I mustn't stay long—my ship is only passing here, but seeing you all was too much for me.

DAME. And very nice too. But, before you go— come on you others, don't stand there looking like last year's calendars—let's give him a good send-off.

They go into :—

No. 16. ENSEMBLE .. .. (FULL COMPANY)

(*During the refrain* JOLIJAK *goes up C., on the bank. At the end, all escort him off R., the* DAME *being last. She stoops to pick up her bathing cap, which she*

*had thrown in the air and dropped. Then she stands
in horror as something appears to have "given" at the
back of her costume. She beckons frantically to
CLARENCE, who tries to "do her up"—finally he wraps
a large towel round her and leads her off. She does the
walk of an Eastern woman, with the pail on her
shoulder, other hand on hip, etc.)*

(SLOW MUSIC. *Enter* BARON HUGO *and* SKRIBB *at* L.,
stealthily.)

BARON. Skribb ! I feel certain we are on the track !
SKRIBB. If not, my lord, we'd best be getting back.
BARON. Back ? Never ! Till I've captured those
          two young 'uns,
          And dragged them safely back into my
          dungeons.
SKRIBB. My Lord ! I hear the strains of happy
          laughter !
          I guess that is the family that we're after !

(*They crawl behind a rock up* L., *and peer over, gazing* R.)

BARON. Yes ! There they are ! Both of 'em !
SKRIBB. C'est tout !
BARON. That's what I said, all two of them are
there.
SKRIBB. Quick, my lord ! Summon our forces !
BARON (*shouting*). Ho, there ! (*Then, to* SKRIBB.)
Are they disguised ?
SKRIBB. Well and truly ! They come !

(MUSIC. SKRIBB *emerges and comes to* C., *the* BARON
following. SKRIBB *beckons to off* L. *Enter* OGBERT
and EGBERT, *covered with a camouflage to disguise
them as a sandbank.*)

BARON (C.). Yes—that will do ! Stand there !
OGBERT (*peeping out*). What are we queueing for ?
EGBERT. Shut up ! We're not queueing—we're
something under the counter !
BARON. Peace, fools ! (*To* SKRIBB.) Come—hide—
we must not be seen. (*To* OGBERT *and* EGBERT.)

Soldiers ! Remain concealed. We shall be back ere long. There is someone approaching. Say nothing ! Do nothing !

(He drags Skribb *off up L.)*

Egbert *(puts head up).* It's all very well to say " Say nothing—do nothing."

Ogbert. Yes—he hasn't got to walk about disguised as a harvest festival.

Egbert. Hush ! Bob down ! He was quite right *(pointing R.)* Look, brother !

Ogbert. Oh—I say ! *(They both hide under their " sandbank.")*

(Enter Lilli *and* Skinna, *R.)*

Lilli. Well—now that Ma's paddling, we can have a bit of a rest.

Skinna. Yes—I'm going to have a sun-bath !

(Comic alarm of Egbert *and* Ogbert *wobbling the "sandbank.")*

Lilli. Splendid ! Yes—here—on this lovely bank !

(They fling off wraps and sit down on the " bank," which collapses.)

Lilli *and* Skinna *(together).* Oh ! Oh !

*(*Ogbert *and* Egbert *emerge.)*

Egbert. Ladies ! Ladies !
Ogbert. Fear nothing !

(They fan the girls with towels.)

Lilli. But what are you ?

Egbert. The brothers Vesuvius. Earthquakes a speciality.

Ogbert. Don't frighten the poor things. *(To the girls.)* We're the army on manœuvres.

Skinna. Manœuvres ?

Egbert. Yes—we were taking cover.

Lilla. Taking cover ?

Egbert. Yes—it's a thing you ladies don't worry about nowadays.

Lilli. Of course—if you're going to be insulting—

OGBERT. Insulting ? The idea's ridiculous ! Excuse me !

EGBERT. Absurd ! Begging your pardon !

SKINNA. Oh, well, if you're sorry, of course, that's different. (*She whispers aside with* LILLI.)

OGBERT. It's all right, brother. They like the look of us.

EGBERT. Yes—because they think you're my brother.

LILLI *and* SKINNA (*together*). Well, we must be going . . .

OGBERT *and* EGBERT (*together*). Oh, NO !

OGBERT. Besides, you were just going to sit down . .

EGBERT. On us—we *love* it !

LILLI. Well—maybe—for a little while . . .

SKINNA. If you're very good . . .

They go into :—

No. 17.   QUARTETTE   ..   (LILLI, SKINNA, OGBERT, EGBERT.)

(*After last refrain . . .* DANCE.)

(*After the Number, a hunting horn, faintly, off.*)

OGBERT (*looking off L.*). Brother ! He's coming back !

EGBERT. What ? Hugo ?

OGBERT. You'll excuse us, ladies—but we've got to get back to the bank.

LILLI. The bank ? You said you were soldiers !

EGBERT. So we are—but if we don't get back to the bank, we shall be cashiered !

DAME'S VOICE (*off R.*). Lilli ! Skinna !

GIRLS. Our mother ! We must go !

BARON'S VOICE (*off L.*). Ho, there !

OGBERT *and* EGBERT. Our Baron ! We must hide !

(LILLI *and* SKINNA *run off R.* OGBERT *and* EGBERT *lie down, hiding under their " sandbank."*)

(JOLIJAK *runs on up C., waving good-bye to those behind him, and shouting "* Good-bye ! Good-bye."

He exits up L., *as the* DAME, DIB, DOLLY, *the children and some of the chorus follow him on up* R., *come down, and group around the stage.)*

DAME. He's gone! He's gone! What a dreadful parting, as the man said who only had two hairs left! My boy! My son! To think he started as an A.B., and now he's gone to sea!

(LOUD MUSIC. *The* BARON *enters* L., *with* SKRIBB.)

BARON. Woman! At last I've found you!
DAME. Good gracious! Where's Clarence? This must be one of my has-beens! (*Sees who it is.*) Mercy! It's the Baron!
DIB *and* DOLLY. Uncle Hugo!
BARON. Yes, dears! Your Uncle—come to rescue you and take you home again.
DAME. Never! (*She stands in front of the* BABES.)
BARON. What did you say?
DAME. I said "never," old man—and when I say "never," I mean—

(CLARENCE *comes on at the back with a huge starfish.*)

CLARENCE. I say—has anybody lost a starfish?
DAME. Oh—you chatterbox! Now—here's my husband—what have you to say to *that*?
BARON. Nothing! Nor to you! You're a pair of kidnappers!
DAME. Oh—are we? When I look at your face, I'm tempted to do a bit of smash and grab.
BARON. Give me those children, or my men will surround you.
DAME. I'd like to see any man surround *me*. And— where are they, pray?
BARON. They are—there!

(EGBERT *and* OGBERT *fling off the " sandbank.*")

ALL (*alarmed*). Oh! Oh!
SKRIBB. And there are hundreds of us—waiting to spring on you.

DAME. Oh! Oh! Clarence—hold me! This is what comes of sunbathing—I knew we should have the beach inspectors after us.

BARON. Now—am I to give the signal for the attack?

DIB *and* DOLLY (*together*). No—no! (*They spring forward to C.*)

DAME. Oh, this is terrible!

DIB. Uncle, you shall not hurt them!

DOLLY. No! We will come back with you!

DAME. Oh, Clarence! That's torn it!

BARON. My darling children! (*Embracing them.*) All is well! Go to my nice kind servants!

(*The* BABES *go to* EGBERT *and* OGBERT, *who smirk and stand on either side of them.*)

(*To* DAME.) Let this be a lesson to you not to meddle with things that don't concern you. . . .

DAME. Dib and Dolly—come back at once!

(*The* BABES *make to go back, but the* BARON *turns to them.*)

BARON. Come, darling children—this woman is evil!

DAME. What!

(BARON, BABES, EGBERT *and* OGBERT *move L.*)

BARON (*turning at the L. exit*). And what is worse —common!

(*The* DAME *collapses in* CLARENCE'S *arms. They fall. Exeunt* BARON, BABES, OGBERT *and* EGBERT.)

SKRIBB (*shouting at the* DAME). Common! And low!

(*The* DAME *struggles up and tries to attack* SKRIBB, *but* CLARENCE *holds her back.*)

(*Exit* SKRIBB *L., cackling with laughter.*)

DAME. Oh, if I could get at him! (*To* CLARENCE.) Why didn't you throw him out?

CLARENCE. I don't like violence !

DAME. A-a-ah !

LILLI. Oh, ma ! Why did you let them go ?

SKINNA. Those two lovely soldiers !

CHILDREN (*crowding round*). Yes, ma ! Yes, ma ! Why did you let them go ?

DAME. Oh, don't screech at me—I'm all of a doo-da ! Oh, if only Jolijak hadn't gone away !

(MUSIC. *Re-enter* JOLIJAK *in great haste up* L. *He comes down* L.C.)

JOLIJAK. Mother ! Where are those children going ?

DAME. Who ? These ?

JOLIJAK. No, no ! Dib and Dolly—with those men !

DAME (*weeping*). They've gone ! They've gone !

JOLIJAK. But where ?

DAME. Back to the Castle with their wicked Uncle !

JOLIJAK. What !

CHILDREN. Oh, Jolijak ! Can't you do *anything?*

JOLIJAK. Of course ! I know he means to do the Babes no good—

DAME. That's why his servants tried to lose them in the wood —

JOLIJAK. Had I been here. I would have thrashed the lordly drunkard.

DAME. But as you weren't, the fact remains, we're bunkered !

CHILDREN. Oh, Jolijak !

JOLIJAK. Not so ! My ship's at hand ! The sails are taut !

> We yet will bring the Baron's schemes to naught !
> My captain's not to any voyage bound me
> So, all aboard, those who will rally round me !

(*He goes up* C. *The others go up and group around him.*)

> Back to our land we sail to fight those knaves !
> For Britons never, never shall be slaves !

(*If practicable, a ship moves in above the bank up stage, in full sail, and all crowd on.   Alternatively, a general grouping around* JOLIJAK.)

ALL *cheer, and go into a reprise of refrain of No.* 16, *or a rousing chorus, at the end of which* . . .

(TABS CLOSE.)

END OF ACT TWO.

ACT THREE.

Scene 1.

Scene.—*The Castle Gates. NIGHT.*

(This may be a cut cloth well down stage. It should have small window cuts R.C. and L.C. A dark arched entrance at C., the backing being an iron gate, or heavy doors.)

When the curtain rises, horses' hoofs are heard and shouts, and jangle of harness, etc.

The Baron *strides on, followed by the* Babes. Skribb, Ogbert *and* Egbert *follow the* Babes.

Baron (*to L.C.*). Home at last ! (*He turns to the* Men). Go, my villains, and prepare all as I have bid you !

Ogbert *and* Egbert. We will ! Away !

(They exit C. Skribb moves up to the Babes.)

Skribb. And I'll get you a nice little supper ! He-he-he !

(Cackling with laughter, exits C. also.)

Baron. Ha ha ! My pretty ones ! Your kind Uncle has you home at last ! You shall sleep soundly to-night !

Dib. Oh, dear—I'm so tired.

Dolly. I never want to ride a horse again.

Dib. Never mind, dear. You did it very well—for a woman. And we'll be all right in the morning.

Dolly. Oh—uncle ! How grim that gate looks !

Baron Nonsense, my dear ! It's there to guard you from all the people outside.

Dolly. 1—I think I'd rather be with the people outside.

Baron. You're tired, the pair of you. Run along, and have some supper.

(*The* BABES *exit at C., through the arch. Immediately afterwards a heavy iron door is heard to clang off. The* BARON *strides down R., with a triumphant laugh.*)

BARON. A joyous sound—the clanging of the gates !

(*The* BABES *appear at the window of the arch.*)

DIB. Uncle !

DOLLY. Oh, Uncle, we're shut in !

BARON. My foolish men have closed the gate too soon ! But you are safe, my pets !

DIB. Yes—safe—but like birds in a cage.

BARON. Nonsense—nonsense. Run along—your supper is waiting.

DOLLY (*tearfully*). I—I—don't want any supper.

DIB (*sternly*). Dolly—don't be childish.

DOLLY. Well—you're crying, too.

DIB. Come *away*, I tell you.

(*They disappear.*)

(*B.O. below window.*)

BARON (*calling*). Skribb ! Skribb !

(SKRIBB *enters C.*)

SKRIBB. Yes, master ?

BARON. They—are—in !

SKRIBB. In ! Ha ! Ha ! That is good !

BARON. When will they be—out ?

SKRIBB. When will they be—*out* ? Ah—that is a good joke !

They go into :—

No. 18. *Villainous Duet and Dance* .. (BARON *and* SKRIBB)

END OF SCENE 1.

At end of Number : CLOSE TABS.

During Scene change :—

Extra verse, refrain, and dance in front of tabs.

Act Three. Scene 2.

Scene.—*The interior of the* Doodrop Inn.

(*Interior wall across up stage. Bar at L. Entrances R. and L.*)

(*The* Innkeeper *and his* Wife *are busy setting out bottles, cleaning glasses, etc. The* Innkeeper *goes to a window and looks out.*)

Innkeeper. Not much business doing to-night. Nobody about.

Wife. No—hardly worth opening for.

Innkeeper. However, we must obey the law.

(*Clock strikes six.*)

Wife. There's the town clock. Better open the door.

(*The* Innkeeper *unbolts the door R., and the* Dame *falls in. She picks herself up.*)

Dame. My word—you are punctual. I was just having a quiet lean—however, now I *am* here—

Innkeeper. What can we do for you ?

Dame (*looking at the bottles*). What a question—with a stock like that. However—now I am here—I want one large bed and four dozen breakfasts. You see— I've brought my family with me.

Wife. Oh—indeed—is it a large family ?

Dame. Yes—the family—the whole family—and nothing but the family—complete with husband. (*calling*) CLARENCE !

(Clarence *runs in R.*)

Clarence. Yes, my dear ?

Dame. This is the old man. He'll settle the details. He's very keen on a bargain—that's why he picked me up.

INKEEPER. Will you be staying long, madam?

DAME. Well—no. We're on our way to the Castle.

INNKEEPER. The Castle! Oh—excuse me! (*bustling round.*) Pray be seated. Maria! Fetch the lady and gentleman some refreshment.

WIFE (*bringing two tankards*). This is indeed a pleasure. (*She gives a tankard to each.*)

DAME. Let's taste it first. (*She drinks and hands her tankard to* CLARENCE.) Hold this a minute, Clarence. You know how these table waters go to your head.

(*She takes his tankard and drinks.*)

CLARENCE. What are your terms?

DAME. Be quiet, Clarence. How many times have I told you not to speak when I'm drinking. (*To the* INNKEEPER.) You can put us up, I suppose?

INNKEEPER. Why—with the greatest of pleasure.

DAME. O.K. (*calling*) Jolijak! Bring in the family!

(CHORUS *of* CHILDREN *troop on, headed by* JOLIJAK. INNKEEPER *and* WIFE *throw up their arms in alarm and hide behind the bar.*)

INNKEEPER. But this isn't a family! It's a revolution!

JOLIJAK (*springing on a chair*). One word with you! Do you know the Baron Hugo?

INNKEEPER *and* WIFE (*together*). Why, yes—we do!

JOLIJAK. Do you like him?

INNKEEPER *and* WIFE. Er—well—

JOLIJAK.   That's quite enough. I understand.
            That man is feared on every hand.
            Within his castle—do you listen?
            He's locked two babes that are not his'n,
            And we've all sworn to set them free,
            Before he tries the Third Degree,
            So that explains without palaver,
            Why we have come to your bar parlour.
            Now—shall we let those children go?
            Come! Everybody answers—

ALL (*including the audience*).   NO !

JOLIJAK. So, all we've got to do to-night,
Is, arm ourselves—then to the fight !

They go into :—

No. 19. DRILLING BALLET   (*with song if desired, and
chorus refrain.*)

(*If practicable, tankards may be used as helmets, the beer
barrel as a drum, and large wine bottles as rifles, etc.*)

(TABS CLOSE.)

END OF SCENE 2.

During Scene change :—

Reprise refrain and routine steps in front of tabs.

Act Three.   Scene 3.

Scene.—*The* Castle Walls, *as in Scene* 1.

(Dolly *is seen alone at the window, looking out.*)

Dolly. Dib! Dib! Where are you? Don't leave me alone!

Dib (*appearing at the window*). I'm here, Dolly. You needn't worry. But I just had an idea.

Dolly. An idea? To escape?

Dib. Yes. I thought we might slide down the waterpipe.

Dolly. Oh—and can we?

Dib. No.

Dolly. Oh—why not?

Dib. 'Cos there isn't any waterpipe.

Dolly. Oh—it does seem cruel—and I'm getting frightened.

Dib. Frightened? Oh—pooh!

Dolly. That's because you're brave.

Dib. I'll always be brave, dear—while I have you to look after. While *I'm* here, you're not to worry.

Dolly. Dib—what's that? Is the moon coming up?

Dib. I don't think even the moon could come up those awful stairs we have to climb.

Dolly. Then—what's that strange light? Oh—Dib!

Dib. Hush!

(*The* Fairy *appears in a blue light.*)

Fairy. Dear children, do not let your hearts beat quicker
　　　Nor let your courage for a moment flicker.
　　　You have been brave, and so deserve the best,
　　　And as for me—well, Fairies *never* rest!
　　　To-night I'll aid your faithful friends attack

And that will be the end of Baron Bacque.
When I have brought him to a deep repen-
    tance
With one short syllable—he'll end your
    sentence.
DIB.   You mean—he'll let us go ?
DOLLY.   Oh, make it soon, for I do fear him so !
FAIRY.   It all depends on Jolijak—and me !
So keep your peckers up—and we shall see !

The FAIRY *goes into :—*

No. 20.   *Song*   ..   ..   (FAIRY)

(DIB *and* DOLLY *join in the refrain.*)

(*The lighting fades slowly to B.O. as the Number ends.*)

TABS CLOSE.

END OF SCENE 3.

ACT THREE.   SCENE 4.

SCENE.—*The* CASTLE COURTYARD. (*As in Act* 1, *Sc.* 1.)

(*It is night. The* BARON *is striding to and fro, furiously, in a spot of moonlight.*)

BARON. What can I do ? Tormented day and night!
        And what may happen to me, ere the
        morning light ?
(*Shouts*) SKRIBB !

        (SKRIBB *rushes on up L.*)

SKRIBB.   Yes, master ?
BARON.   Skribb—you got me into this ! You must
get me out !
SKRIBB.   I—master ?
BARON.   Yes ! Don't stand there and call me master !
You have mastered me !
SKRIBB.   I ?
BARON.   Didn't you read that beastly manuscript
about the Babes—and all their money ?
SKRIBB.   Only, my lord, because you cannot read.
BARON.   No—and I wish you couldn't, either.
Oh—when I think of those children—and all that
money—and then—to wait twenty years ! Oh !
SKRIBB.   You would rather think of the money—
without the children—eh ?
BARON. If I could ! If I could !
SKRIBB.   There might be a way !
BARON. A way ?
SKRIBB.   Yes—if you tell me to send the Babes
away. You need not enquire—where they have gone.
BARON. But—the manuscript ?
SKRIBB.   We will prepare another manuscript—on
slightly different lines. It shall be done by a skilful
attorney.
BARON.   An attorney ? Can we find one ?

SKRIBB. With all speed. It is a long lane that has no attorney.

BARON. Skribb—if this is done—

SKRIBB. 'Twere well 'twere done quickly. I go—but to return with an attorney.

(*He exits L.*)

BARON (*turning runs R.C.*). Dare we do it? So much wrong? For so much money? Yes!

(*Bells heard off. Then, in a blue spot, the fairy appears through the wall, up C.*)

FAIRY. Why, no—you dare not!

BARON (*turning*). Who speaks—who says I dare not?

FAIRY. I speak—and by my fairy art,
　　Will bring to you a change of heart.
　　Come—drop at once these schemes malevolent,
　　'Tis time that you became benevolent.

BARON. Fool! Fairy! Phantom! What you be,
　　A change of heart's no use to me.
　　Be off—a foolish errand thine,
　　A fairy's no affair of mine.

FAIRY. You wretched man, entwined in evil,
　　You're no more human than a weevil,
　　But yet, I'll give you one more chance,
　　Release those Babes and I will grant
　　You health and happiness for years,
　　While they enjoy what's rightly theirs.

BARON. What's rightly *mine*! If I can snatch it!
　　Begone! Avaunt! Or else—you'll catch it!
　　(*He threatens her with his sword.*)

FAIRY. Rash man! I'll tell you at this juncture,
　　You can't with sword a fairy puncture.
　　But, since you will not heed my chiding,
　　I'll see that you receive a hiding.

BARON. Oh, really? When will they begin it?

FAIRY. Rash man! Almost this very minute!
　　(*She disappears through the wall.*)

BARON. But—zounds and confusion! Skribb!

(SKRIBB *runs on.*)

Who was that person you allowed to enter?

SKRIBB. No one, master!

BARON. No one? But—there *was* someone!

SKRIBB. I heard—nothing. I saw—nothing.

BARON. Fool! Can I have imagined it?

SKRIBB. No, master—you can imagine nothing.

BARON. I'll be tricked no longer! Fetch me the Babes!

(*As daylight slowly fades in.*)

The morning comes! My fortunes still elude me!
All I have now are vain hopes to delude me!

SKRIBB. Not so, master! I have yet a plan (*He whispers to the* BARON, *who gasps.*) It is better it should be over—quickly! (*He exits L.*)

BARON. Yes! Yes! Quickly! I have been weak to let so much wealth stand within my grasp—and fail to grasp it.

(DIB *and* DOLLY *enter L. with* SKRIBB, *who then slyly exits.*)

DIB. You sent for us, Uncle Hugo?

BARON. Yes! Stand there, you treacherous infants! You have been false and treasonous!

DIB *and* DOLLY (*together*). Oh—no—no—uncle!

BARON. Silence! I say you have been false and I must punish you.

DIB (*stepping forward*). Uncle—you have no right—you're frightening my sister.

BARON. Quiet, boy. I am merciful. I shall not kill you—yet. I shall only fine you. Your money is yours no longer.

DOLLY. Oh—Dib! Dib!

DIB. Uncle—you are Uncle no longer. Take our money if you will—and we will go!

BARON. Go? To spread tales? Never!

DIB. What do you mean?

BARON. I mean—just what I say !

(*Uproar heard off L. Crashes and shouts.* SKRIBB *rushes on from L.*)

SKRIBB. Master—you are in danger ! There is a raging army at the gates !

BARON. A raging army ?

(EGBERT *and* OGBERT *rush on L.*)

EGBERT. Raging army ? Why—it's the whole Army and Navy Stores !

OGBERT. Oh—it's terrible ! They'll have the gates down in a minute !

EGBERT. Yes—I've never seen anything like it, since Aston Villa played the M.C.C.

BARON. What does it mean ?

(*Crash off.*)

OGBERT. Oh—there goes the scullery window !

(MUSIC. JOLIJAK *rushes on L., with a sword.*)

JOLIJAK. Ah ! At last ! The Baron !

BARON. Out of my way ! I cannot bear the sight of you !

JOLIJAK. Then close your eyes—for ever !

EGBERT. A-ow ! Look out ! This is a personal matter !

(OGBERT *and* EGBERT *drag the* BABES *up C.* SKRIBB *cowers behind the bench down R.* MUSIC *during a duel between* JOLIJAK *and the* BARON, *at the end of which the* BARON *is wounded and sinks to the ground.*)

JOLIJAK. Conquered ! The tyrant bows his head ! Who's next ?

SKRIBB. Not me !

EGBERT *and* OGBERT. Not us !

(DAME TRUFORM *rushes on* L., *followed by the* CHILDREN, INNKEEPER *and his* WIFE.)

DAME. Jolijak ! Are you alive ? Oh yes, I see you are !

JOLIJAK. Mother—it is over !

DAME. All right—then change the bowling.

(VILLAGERS, *etc.*, *enter* R. *and group.* The FAIRY *appears up* C.)

FAIRY. One moment ! All is over—with my slight assistance.

But pardon me if I now show polite insistence

On punishing the Baron and his fellow,

Whom you see there, now turning very yellow !

(*They all look at* BARON *and* SKRIBB *down* R.)

Both must go hiking, all alone, for twenty years

To make sure nothing of this kind again occurs !

Away ! Unless you care to join the final chorus !

BARON. I think we will—there's nothing better for us.

FAIRY. Come forward, Babes ! You need no longer hide !

These kindly folk your future will decide.

DAME. I know ! I'll co-opt them into my family !

DIB. And you shall all live in the Castle with us !

DOLLY. Oh, lovely !

JOLIJAK. And when you're old enough, I shall marry you !

DOLLY. Oh, lovely !

LILLI (*pointing at* OGBERT *and* EGBERT). Ooh, ma ! Those are the two gentlemen we met on the beach !

(LILLI *and* SKINNA *run over to* OGBERT *and* EGBERT.)

DAME.   What ! (*shouting*) Clarence !

(CLARENCE *enters L., with spear and shield.*)

CLARENCE.   Am I too late ?

DAME.   Yes, as usual.

(OGBERT *and* EGBERT *have their arms round the two girls.*)

CLARENCE.   Oh. Good.

DAME.   Go and ask those two men their intentions.

CLARENCE (*seeing the situation*).   Do you think it necessary, dear ? What can we do about it ?

DAME.   Well—if you ask me, I'm going to have a word with the orchestra !

(ALL *form a stage picture for the Finale.*)

No. 21.   FINAL CHORUS   ..   *Full Company.*

(*Popular refrains and refrains in the show, and dance as the curtain falls.*)

CURTAIN.

FURNITURE AND PROPERTY PLOT.

ACT 1.

SCENE 1.

Two or three small benches.
Small garden table.   A stool.

Props. :
Merchandise for Tradespeople.
Staves for Ogbert and Egbert.
Mugs and cake for Babes.

SCENE 2.

Wooden stile.
Posts and rope.   (*For fight ring.   Not essential.*)

Props. :
Bag of blackberries.   (BABES.)
Packet of Sandwiches.   (OGBERT *and* EGBERT.)

SCENE 3.

Grass-covered bank.   Trick thistle, spider's web, etc.

Props. :
Leaves to fall for ROBIN BALLET.
Some large pieces of gauze, with leaves sewn on, to cover Babes by the robins.

SCENE 4.

Table, and chair.   *On it :* Inkstand and quill.

Props. :
Manuscript. (SKRIBB.)

SCENE 5.

Two or three large mushrooms, set during previous Scene.

Act 2.

Scene 1.

The Shoe. Gang-plank leading to the same.
Tripod, fire. Long low bench. Two stools.

Props.:

Frying-pan. Kettle (*N.B. Siren effect off.*)
Rashers of bacon. One trick rasher.
Set of trick plates.
Loaf of bread cut in slices and packed close to have
appearance of an uncut loaf.
Punting poles. Length of rope.

Scene 2.

Bottle of buttercup wine. (Dame.)

Scene 4.

No additional props.

Scene 5.

Staves or swords (Ogbert *and* Egbert).
Heavy camouflage hessian sheet, painted to look like
a sandbank. (Ogbert *and* Egbert.)
Spade and pail. Huge starfish. Towel. (Clarence.

Act 3.

Scene 1.

Prop: Manuscript (Skribb).

Scene 2.

Bar counter. Bench. Chair. Two stools.
Small cask. Several tankards. Bottles, etc.

Scene 3.

Nil.

Scene 4.

Staves (Ogbert *and* Egbert).
Swords. (Baron *and* Jolijak.)
Comic spear and shield. (Clarence.)

EFFECTS.

Hunting horn. Fairy Bells. Owl.

Iron gate clang. Crashes.

————

NOTES ON LIGHTING.

All the major scenes should be brightly lit throughout the show. Floats and battens should be amber and white, full, with any F.O.H. flooding which may be available. The occasions where lighting should be dimmed, and some special spotting made, are indicated in the script, such as the night scenes in the wood, and the Baron's study. The scenes at the Castle Gates, also, should be dimmed somewhat, and a central pool of deep amber light introduced. This is faded out when the Fairy is spotted in a blue pool.

The light behind the barred window on the Babes should be pale blue.

It should be noted that there are some snap B.O.s at the end of some of the scenes.